Books by Mark Strand

Poetry

Dark Harbor   1993
The Continuous Life   1990
Selected Poems   1980
The Late Hour   1978
The Story of Our Lives   1973
Darker   1970
Reasons for Moving   1968
Sleeping with One Eye Open   1964

Prose

Mr. and Mrs. Baby   1985
The Monument   1978

Translations

Travelling in the Family   1986
(Poems by Carlos Drummond de Andrade, with Thomas Colchie)
The Owl's Insomnia   1973
(Poems by Raphael Alberti)

Art Books

William Bailey   1987
Art of the Real   1983
Hopper   1994

For Children

The Planet of Lost Things   1982
The Night Book   1985
Rembrandt Takes A Walk   1986

Anthologies

Another Republic (with Charles Simic)   1976
New Poetry of Mexico (with Octavio Paz)   1970
The Contemporary American Poets   1969
The Golden Ecco Anthology   1994

THE GOLDEN ECCO ANTHOLOGY

100 Great Poems
of the English Language

❏

Edited by
MARK STRAND

THE ECCO PRESS

Selection and Preface copyright © 1994 by Mark Strand
All poems not in the public domain are reprinted by permission
All rights reserved

THE ECCO PRESS
100 West Broad Street
Hopewell, New Jersey 08525
Published simultaneously in Canada by
Penguin Books Canada Ltd., Ontario
Printed in the United States of America
Designed by Debby Jay

FIRST EDITION

Library of Congress Cataloging-in-Publication Data

The golden ecco anthology: 100 great poems of the English language /
edited by Mark Strand. – 1st ed.
p.   cm.
1. English poetry.   2. American poetry.   I. Strand, Mark, 1934–
PR1175.G5563   1994
821.008 – dc20   94-25449
ISBN 0-88001-366-4

The text of this book is set in Cochin
Pages 177 through 180 constitute a continuation of this page

Errata

page 64:

ROBERT BURNS

(1759-1796, Scottish)

page 70:

WALTER SCOTT

(1771-1832, Scottish)

page 109:

WILLIAM BUTLER YEATS

(1865-1939, Irish)

CONTENTS

PREFACE

Most poets keep a mental list of their favorite poems, which is revised from time to time when a new poem or newly discovered poem replaces one of the favorites. *The Golden Ecco Anthology* is a distillation of my list as it currently stands – a list within a list, an inner circle. For a poem to be on the list it must have remained an undiminished source of pleasure over innumerable readings and set such a high standard of technical accomplishment that it seems as much an object of wonder as it does a form of communication.

A poet's list of poems is a good deal more fluid than an anthology derived from the list would make it appear. That is, the public nature of an anthology demands considerations beyond what does or does not delight its editor. *The Golden Ecco Anthology*, though drawn from my own list of favorite poems, makes some concessions to what I think will please an audience unused to reading poetry. The principles of selection were simple, but difficult to enact. I wanted to include one hundred poets, and a single poem for each. I also wanted the poem to be short, if possible. If I liked two poems equally by the same author, the nod would go to the shorter one. This explains, for example, my selection of Whitman's "A Noiseless Patient Spider" over several much longer poems of his that I like just as much. In cases where I had to choose from many poems of the same length, as in the sonnet sequence of Spenser or Shakespeare, or in the poems of Emily Dickinson, it was difficult, and the determining factor became the relative accessibility of the particular poem on a first or second reading. The decision to include more American poets than British poets from the mid-nineteenth century onward was based not only on my preference for recent

American poetry, but on the likelihood that readers of this book will be American and therefore might be drawn to poets whose immediate experience of the world more closely resembles their own.

This is a book to be read casually—a poem or two at a sitting. It does not present poems as documents to be studied or puzzles to be solved. I believe that good poems, because they are answerable to our humanness, whether broadly or narrowly considered, are always relevant and have for the most part no need of critical or biographical assistance. The poems in *The Golden Ecco Anthology* are meant to be enjoyed.

M.S.

THE GOLDEN ECCO
ANTHOLOGY

ANONYMOUS

(13th–15th century, British)

———

Fowls in the Frith

Fowles in the frith,
The fisshes in the flood,
And I mon waxe wood:
Much sorwe I walke with
For beste of boon and blood.

ANONYMOUS

(13th–15th century, British)

———

I Am of Ireland

Ich am of Irlonde,
And of the holy londe
   Of Irlonde.
Goode sire, praye ich thee,
For of sainte charitee,
Com and dance with me
   In Irlonde.

ANONYMOUS

(13th–15th century, British)

———

Thomas the Rhymer

True Thomas lay on Huntlie bank,
  A ferlie he spied wi' his ee,
And there he saw a lady bright,
  Come riding down by the Eildon Tree.

Her shirt was o the grass-green silk,
  Her mantle o the velvet fyne,
At ilka tett of her horse's mane
  Hang fifty siller bells and nine.

True Thomas, he pulld aff his cap,
  And louted low down to his knee:
'All hail, thou mighty Queen of Heaven!
  For thy peer on earth I never did see.'

'O no, O no, Thomas,' she said,
  'That name does not belang to me;
I am but the queen of fair Elfland,
  That am hither come to visit thee.

'Harp and carp, Thomas,' she said,
  'Harp and carp along wi me,
And if ye dare to kiss my lips,
  Sure of your bodie I will be.'

'Betide me weal, betide me woe,
    That weird shall never daunton me;'
Syne he has kissed her rosy lips,
    All underneath the Eildon Tree.

'Now, ye maun go wi me,' she said,
    'True Thomas, ye maun go wi me,
And ye maun serve me seven years,
    Thro weal or woe, as may chance to be.'

She mounted on her milk-white steed,
    She's taen True Thomas up behind,
And aye wheneer her bridle rung,
    The steed flew swifter than the wind.

O they rade on, and farther on —
    The steed gaed swifter than the wind —
Untill they reached a desart wide,
    And living land was left behind.

'Light down, light down, now, True Thomas,
    And lean your head upon my knee;
Abide and rest a little space,
    And I will show you ferlies three.

'O see ye not yon narrow road,
    So thick beset with thorns and briers?
That is the path of righteousness,
    Tho after it but few enquires.

'And see not ye that braid braid road,
    That lies across that lily leven?
That is the path of wickedness,
    Tho some call it the road to heaven.

'And see not ye that bonny road,
    That winds about the fernie brae?
That is the road to fair Elfland,
    Where thou and I this night maun gae.

'But, Thomas, ye maun hold your tongue,
    Whatever ye may hear or see,
For, if you speak word in Elflyn land,
    Ye'll neer get back to your ain countrie.'

O they rade on, and farther on,
    And they waded thro rivers aboon the knee,
And they saw neither sun nor moon,
    But they heard the roaring of the sea.

It was mirk mirk night, and there was nae stern light,
    And they waded thro red blude to the knee;
For a' the blude that's shed on earth
    Rins thro the springs o that countrie.

Syne they came on to a garden green,
    And she pu'd an apple frae a tree:
'Take this for thy wages, True Thomas,
    It will give the tongue that can never lie.'

'My tongue is mine ain,' True Thomas said;
    'A gudely gift we wad gie to me!
I neither dought to buy nor sell,
    At fair or tryst where I may be.

'I dought neither speak to prince or peer,
    Nor ask of grace from fair ladye:'
'Now hold thy peace,' the lady said,
    'For as I say, so must it be.'

He has gotten a coat of the even cloth,
  And a pair of shoes of velvet green,
And till seven years were gane and past
  True Thomas on earth was never seen.

ANONYMOUS

(13th–15th century, British)

———

Sir Patrick Spens

The king sits in Dumferline town,
   Drinking the blude-reid wine:
"O whar will I get a guid sailor
   To sail this ship of mine?"

Up and spak an eldern knicht,
   Sat at the king's richt knee:
"Sir Patrick Spens is the best sailor
   That sails upon the sea."

The king has written a braid letter
   And signed it wi' his hand,
And sent it to Sir Patrick Spens,
   Was walking on the sand.

The first line that Sir Patrick read,
   A loud lauch lauched he;
The next line that Sir Patrick read,
   The tear blinded his ee.

"O wha is this has done this deed,
   This ill deed done to me,
To send me out this time o' the year,
   To sail upon the sea?

"Make haste, make haste, my mirry men all,
   Our guid ship sails the morn."
"O say na sae, my master dear,
   For I fear a deadly storm.

"Late late yestre'en I saw the new moon
   Wi' the auld moon in her arm,
And I fear, I fear, my dear master,
   That we will come to harm."

O our Scots nobles were richt laith
   To weet their cork-heeled shoon,
But lang owre a' the play were played
   Their hats they swam aboon.

O lang, lang may their ladies sit,
   Wi' their fans into their hand,
O e'er they see Sir Patrick Spens
   Come sailing to the land.

O lang, lang may the ladies stand,
   Wi' their gold kembs in their hair,
Waiting for their ain dear lords,
   For they'll see thame na mair.

Half o'er, half o'er to Aberdour
   It's fifty fadom deep,
And there lies guid Sir Patrick Spens,
   Wi' the Scots lords at his feet.

ANONYMOUS

(15th century, British)

———

Western Wind

Westron wind, when will thou blow?
The small rain down can rain.
Christ, that my love were in my arms,
And I in my bed again.

THOMAS WYATT

(1503–1542, British)

They fle from me that sometyme
did me seke

They fle from me that sometyme did me seke
   With naked fote stalking in my chambre.
I have sene theim gentill tame and meke
   That nowe are wyld and do not remembre
   That sometyme they put theimself in daunger
To take bred at my hand; and nowe they raunge
Besely seeking with a continuell chaunge.

Thancked be fortune, it hath ben othrewise
   Twenty tymes better; but ons in speciall,
In thyn arraye after a pleasaunt gyse,
   When her lose gowne from her shoulders did fall,
   And she me caught in her armes long and small;
Therewithall swetely did me kysse,
And softely saide, *dere hert, howe like you this?*

It was no dreme: I lay brode waking.
   But all is torned thorough my gentilnes
Into a straunge fasshion of forsaking;
   And I have leve to goo of her goodenes,
   And she also to vse new fangilnes.
But syns that I so kyndely ame serued,
I would fain knowe what she hath deserued.

GEORGE GASCOIGNE

(1539–1577, British)

The Lullaby of a Lover

Sing lullaby, as women doe,
Wherewith they bring their babes to rest,
And lullaby can I sing to,
As womanly as can the best.
With lullaby they still the childe,
And if I be not much beguild,
Full many wanton babes have I,
Which must be stild with lullabie.

First lullaby my youthfull yeares,
It is nowe time to go to bed,
For croocked age and hoary heares,
Have wone the haven [within] my head:
With Lullaby then youth be still,
With Lullaby content thy will,
Since courage quayles, and commes behind,
Go sleepe, and so beguile thy minde.

Next Lullaby my gazing eyes,
Which wonted were to glaunce apace.
For every Glasse maye nowe suffise,
To shewe the furrowes in my face:
With Lullabye then winke awhile,
With Lullabye your lookes beguile:
Lette no fayre face, nor beautie brighte,
Entice you efte with vayne delighte.

[13]

And Lullaby my wanton will,
Lette reasons rule, nowe reigne thy thought,
Since all to late I finde by skyll,
Howe deare I have thy fansies bought:
With Lullaby nowe tak thyne ease,
With Lullaby thy doubtes appease:
For trust to this, if thou be styll,
 My body shall obey thy will.

Eke Lullaby my loving boye,
My little Robyn take thy rest,
Since age is colde, and nothing coye,
Keepe close thy coyne, for so is best:
With Lulla[b]y be thou content,
With Lullaby thy lustes relente,
Lette others pay which hath mo pence,
Thou art to pore for such expence.

 Thus Lullabye my youth, myne eyes,
My will, my ware, and all that was,
I can no mo delayes devise,
But welcome payne, let pleasure passe:
With Lullaby now take your leave,
With Lullaby your dreames deceive,
And when you rise with waking eye,
Remember then this Lullabye.

Ever or Never.

[14]

BARNABE GOOGE

(1540–1594, British)

———

Of Money

Give money me, take friendship whoso list,
For friends are gone come once adversity,
When money yet remaineth safe in chest,
That quickly can thee bring from misery;
Fair face show friends when riches do abound;
Come time of proof, farewell, they must away;
Believe me well, they are not to be found
If God but send thee once a lowering day.
Gold never starts aside, but in distress,
Finds ways enough to ease thine heaviness.

SIR EDWARD DYER

(1543–1607, British)

———

The Lowest Trees Have Tops

The lowest trees haue topps, the ante her gall,
The flie her spleene, the little sparke his heat:
The slender hears cast shadows, though but small,
And bees haue stinges, although they be not great;
   Seas haue their sourse, and soe haue shallow springes:
   And Loue is Loue, in beggers and in Kinges.

Wher waters smothest ronne, ther deepest are the foords,
The diall stirrs, yet none perceiues it moove;
The firmest fayth is fowned in fewest woordes,
The turtles doe not singe, and yet thye loue;
   True heartes haue ears and eyes, no tongues to speake:
   They heare and see, and sigh, and then they breake.

SIR WALTER RALEGH (RALEIGH)

(1552–1618, British)

─────

The Lie

Goe soule, the bodies guest,
  Upon a thankelesse arrant,
Feare not to touch the best,
  The truth shall be thy warrant:
Goe, since I needs must die,
  And give the world the lie.

Say to the Court it glowes,
  And shines like rotten wood,
Say to the Church it showes
  Whats good, and doth no good.
If Church and Court reply,
  Then give them both the lie.

Tell Potentates they live
  Acting by others action,
Not loved unlesse they give,
  Not strong but by affection.
If Potentates reply,
  Give Potentates the lie.

Tell men of high condition,
  That mannage the estate,
Their purpose is ambition,
  Their practise onely hate:
And if they once reply,
  Then give them all the lie.

Tell them that brave it most,
   They beg for more by spending,
Who in their greatest cost
   Seek nothing but commending.
And if they make replie,
   Then give them all the lie.

Tell zeale it wants devotion,
   Tell love it is but lust,
Tell time it meets but motion,
   Tell flesh it is but dust.
And wish them not replie
   For thou must give the lie.

Tell age it daily wasteth,
   Tell honour how it alters.
Tell beauty how she blasteth
   Tell favour how it falters
And as they doe reply
   Give every one the lie.

Tell wit how much it wrangles
   In tickle points of nycenesse,
Tell wisedome she entangles
   Her selfe in over wisenesse.
And when they doe reply
   Straight give them both the lie.

Tell Phisicke of her boldnes,
   Tell skill it is prevention:
Tell charity of coldnes,
   Tell law it is contention,
And as they doe reply
   So give them still the lie.

Tell fortune of her blindnesse,
    Tell nature of decay,
Tell friendship of unkindnesse,
    Tell justice of delay.
And if they will reply,
    Then give them all the lie.

Tell Arts they have no soundnesse,
    But vary by esteeming,
Tell schooles they want profoundnes
    And stand too much on seeming.
If Arts and schooles reply,
    Give arts and schooles the lie.

Tell faith its fled the Citie,
    Tell how the country erreth,
Tell manhood shakes off pittie,
    Tell vertue least preferreth,
And if they doe reply,
    Spare not to give the lie.

So when thou hast as I
    Commanded thee, done blabbing,
Although to give the lie,
    Deserves no lesse then stabbing,
Stab at thee he that will,
    No stab thy soule can kill.

EDMUND SPENSER

(1552–1599, British)

———

One day I wrote her name upon the strand

One day I wrote her name upon the strand,
But came the waves and washèd it away:
Agayne I wrote it with a second hand,
But came the tyde, and made my paynes his pray.
"Vayne man," sayd she, "that doest in vaine assay,
A mortall thing so to immortalize,
For I my selve shall lyke to this decay,
And eek my name bee wypèd out lykewize."
"Not so," quod I, "let baser things devise,
To dy in dust, but you shall live by fame:
My verse your vertues rare shall eternize,
And in the heavens wryte your glorious name.
Where whenas death shall all the world subdew,
Our love shall live, and later life renew."

SIR PHILIP SIDNEY

(1554–1586, British)

———

Ye Goat-herd Gods

Strephon. Ye Goat-herd gods, that love the grassy
      mountains,
    Ye nymphs which haunt the springs in pleasant
      valleys,
    Ye satyrs joyed with free and quiet forests,
    Vouchsafe your silent ears to plaining music,
    Which to my woes gives still an early morning,
    And draws the dolor on till weary evening.

Klaius. O Mercury, foregoer to the evening,
    O heavenly huntress of the savage mountains,
    O lovely star, entitled of the morning,
    While that my voice doth fill these woeful valleys,
    Vouchsafe your silent ears to plaining music,
    Which oft hath *Echo* tired in secret forests.

Strephon. I that was once free burgess of the forests,
    Where shade from Sun, and sport I sought in
      evening,
    I, that was once esteemed for pleasant music,
    Am banished now among the monstrous mountains
    Of huge despair, and foul affliction's valleys,
    Am grown a screech-owl to myself each morning.

Klaius. I that was once delighted every morning,
    Hunting the wild inhabiters of forests,

I, that was once the music of these valleys,
So darkened am, that all my day is evening,
Heart-broken so, that molehills seem high mountains,
And fill the vales with cries instead of music.

Strephon. Long since alas, my deadly swannish music
Hath made itself a crier of the morning,
And hath with wailing strength climbed highest
mountains;
Long since my thoughts more desert be than forests,
Long since I see my joys come to their evening,
And state thrown down to over-trodden valleys.

Klaius. Long since the happy dwellers of these valleys
Have prayed me leave my strange exclaiming music,
Which troubles their day's work, and joys of evening;
Long since I hate the night, more hate the morning;
Long since my thoughts chase me like beasts in
forests,
And make me wish myself laid under mountains.

Strephon. Meseems I see the high and stately mountains
Transform themselves to low dejected valleys;
Meseems I hear in these ill-changed forests
The nightingales do learn of owls their music;
Meseems I feel the comfort of the morning
Turned to the mortal serene of an evening.

Klaius. Meseems I see a filthy cloudy evening
As soon as sun begins to climb the mountains;
Meseems I feel a noisome scent, the morning
When I do smell the flowers of these valleys;
Meseems I hear, when I do hear sweet music,
The dreadful cries of murdered men in forests.

Strephon. I wish to fire the trees of all these forests;
    I give the sun a last farewell each evening;
    I curse the fiddling finders-out of music;
    With envy I do hate the lofty mountains
    And with despite despise the humble valleys;
    I do detest night, evening, day, and morning.

Klaius. Curse to myself my prayer is, the morning;
    My fire is more than can be made with forests,
    My state more base than are the basest valleys;
    I wish no evenings more to see, each evening;
    Shamèd, I hate myself in sight of mountains
    And stop mine ears, lest I grow mad with music.

Strephon. For she, whose parts maintained a perfect music,
    Whose beauties shined more than the blushing
        morning,
    Who much did pass in state the stately mountains,
    In straightness passed the cedars of the forests,
    Hath cast me, wretch, into eternal evening
    By taking her two suns from these dark valleys.

Klaius. For she, with whom compared, the Alps are
        valleys,
    She, whose least word brings from the spheres their
        music,
    At whose approach the sun rase in the evening,
    Who, where she went, bare in her forehead morning,
    Is gone, is gone from these our spoilèd forests,
    Turning to deserts our best pastured mountains.

Strephon. These mountains witness shall, so shall these
        valleys,
Klaius. These forests eke, made wretched by our music,
    Our morning hymn this is, and song at evening.

[23]

ROBERT SOUTHWELL, S.J.

(1561–1595, British)

———

The Burning Babe

As I in hoary winter's night stood shivering in the snow,
Surprised I was with sudden heat which made my heart to
     glow;
And lifting up a fearful eye to view what fire was near,
A pretty babe all burning bright did in the air appear;
Who, scorchèd with excessive heat, such floods of tears
     did shed
As though his floods should quench his flames which with
     his tears were fed.
"Alas," quoth he, "but newly born in fiery heats I fry,
Yet none approach to warm their hearts or feel my fire
     but I!
My faultless breast the furnace is, the fuel wounding
     thorns,
Love is the fire, and sighs the smoke, the ashes shame and
     scorns;
The fuel justice layeth on, and mercy blows the coals,
The metal in this furnace wrought are men's defilèd souls,
For which, as now on fire I am to work them to their
     good,
So will I melt into a bath to wash them in my blood."
With this he vanished out of sight and swiftly shrunk
     away,
And straight I callèd unto mind that it was Christmas day.

THOMAS NASHE

(1567–1601, British)

A Litany in Time of Plague

Adieu, farewell, earth's bliss;
This world uncertain is;
Fond are life's lustful joys;
Death proves them all but toys;
None from his darts can fly;
I am sick, I must die.
  Lord, have mercy on us!

Rich men, trust not in wealth,
Gold cannot buy you health;
Physic himself must fade.
All things to end are made,
The plague full swift goes by;
I am sick, I must die.
  Lord, have mercy on us!

Beauty is but a flower
Which wrinkles will devour;
Brightness falls from the air;
Queens have died young and fair;
Dust hath closèd Helen's eye.
I am sick, I must die.
  Lord, have mercy on us!

Strength stoops unto the grave,
Worms feed on Hector brave;

Swords may not fight with fate,
Earth still holds ope her gate.
"Come, come!" the bells do cry.
I am sick, I must die.
    Lord, have mercy on us.

Wit with his wantonness
Tasteth death's bitterness;
Hell's executioner
Hath no ears for to hear
What vain art can reply.
I am sick, I must die.
    Lord, have mercy on us.

Haste, therefore, each degree,
To welcome destiny;
Heaven is our heritage,
Earth but a player's stage;
Mount we unto the sky.
I am sick, I must die.
    Lord, have mercy on us.

CHIDIOCK TICHBORNE

(1558–1586, British)

———

Elegy

My prime of youth is but a frost of cares,
  My feast of joy is but a dish of pain,
My crop of corn is but a field of tares,
  And all my good is but vain hope of gain;
    The day is past, and yet I saw no sun,
    And now I live, and now my life is done.

My tale was heard and yet it was not told,
  My fruit is fallen and yet my leaves are green,
My youth is spent and yet I am not old,
  I saw the world and yet I was not seen;
    My thread is cut and yet it is not spun,
    And now I live, and now my life is done.

I sought my death and found it in my womb,
  I looked for life and saw it was a shade,
I trod the earth and knew it was my tomb,
  And now I die, and now I was but made;
    My glass is full, and now my glass is run,
    And now I live, and now my life is done.

MICHAEL DRAYTON

(1563–1631, British)

———

Since ther's no helpe,
come let us kisse and part

Since ther's no helpe, Come let us kisse and part,
Nay, I have done: You get no more of Me,
And I am glad, yea glad with all my heart,
That thus so cleanly, I my Selfe can free,
Shake hands for ever, Cancell all our Vowes,
And when We meet at any time againe,
Be it not seene in either of our Browes,
That We one jot of former Love reteyne;
Now at the last gaspe, of Loves latest Breath,
When his Pulse fayling, Passion speechlesse lies,
When Faith is kneeling by his bed of Death,
And Innocence is closing up his Eyes,
Now if thou would'st, when all have given him over,
From Death to Life, thou might'st him yet recover.

CHRISTOPHER MARLOWE

(1564–1593, British)

———

The Passionate Shepherd to His Love

Come live with mee, and be my love,
And we will all the pleasures prove,
That Vallies, groves, hills and fieldes,
Woods, or steepie mountaine yeeldes.

And wee will sit upon the Rocks,
Seeing the Sheepheards feede theyr flocks
By shallow Rivers, to whose falls
Melodious byrds sings Madrigalls.

And I will make thee beds of Roses,
And a thousand fragrant poesies,
A cap of flowers, and a kirtle,
Imbroydred all with leaves of Mirtle.

A gowne made of the finest wooll,
Which from our pretty Lambes we pull,
Fayre lined slippers for the cold,
With buckles of the purest gold.

A belt of straw and Ivie buds,
With Corall clasps and Amber studs,
And if these pleasures may thee move,
Come live with mee, and be my love.

The Sheepheards Swaines shall daunce & sing
For thy delight each May-morning.
If these delights thy minde may move,
Then live with mee, and be my love.

WILLIAM SHAKESPEARE

(1564–1616, British)

———

How like a winter hath my absence been

How like a winter hath my absence been
From thee, the pleasure of the fleeting year!
What freezings have I felt, what dark days seen!
What old December's bareness everywhere!
And yet this time remov'd was summer's time;
The teeming autumn, big with rich increase,
Bearing the wanton burthen of the prime,
Like widowed wombs after their lords' decease.
Yet this abundant issue seem'd to me
But hope of orphans and unfathered fruit;
For summer and his pleasures wait on thee,
And, thou away, the very birds are mute;
　　Or, if they sing, 'tis with so dull a cheer
　　That leaves look pale, dreading the winter's near.

ANONYMOUS

(17th century, British)

———

Tom O'Bedlam's Song

From the hagg and hungrie goblin
That into raggs would rend ye,
And the spirit that stands by the naked man
In the Book of Moones defend yee!
That of your five sounde sences
You never be forsaken,
Nor wander from your selves with Tom
Abroad to begg your bacon.

> *While I doe sing "ang foode, any feeding,*
> *Feedinge, drinke or clothing,"*
> *Come dame or maid, be not afraid,*
> *Poor Tom will injure nothing.*

Of thirty bare years have I
Twice twenty bin enragèd,
And of forty bin three tymes fifteene
In durance soundlie cagèd.
On the lordlie loftes of Bedlam,
With stubble softe and dainty,
Brave braceletts strong, sweet whips ding-dong,
With wholsome hunger plenty.

> *And nowe I sing, etc.*

With a thought I tooke for Maudlin,
And a cruse of cockle pottage,
With a thing thus tall, skie blesse you all,

I befell into this dotage.
I slept not since the Conquest,
Till then I never wakèd,
Till the rogysh boy of love where I lay
Mee found and strip't mee naked.

And nowe I sing, etc.

When I short have shorne my sowre face
And swigg'd my horny barrel,
In an oaken inne I pound my skin
As a suite of guilt apparell.
The moon's my constant Mistrisse,
And the lowlie owle my morrowe,
The flaming Drake and the Nightcrowe make
Mee musicke to my sorrowe.

While I doe sing, etc.

The palsie plagues my pulses
When I prigg your pigs or pullen,
Your culvers take, or matchles make
Your Chanticleare, or sullen.
When I want provant with Hunfrie
I sup, and when benighted,
I repose in Powles with waking soules
Yet nevere am affrighted.

But I doe sing, etc.

I knowe more then Apollo,
For oft, when hee ly's sleeping,
I see the starres att bloudie warres
In the wounded welkin weeping;
The moone embrace her shepheard,
And the quene of Love her warryor,
While the first doth borne the star of morne,

And the next the heavenly Farrier.

While I doe sing, etc.

The Gipsie Snap and Pedro
Are none of Tom's comradoes.
The punk I skorne and the cut purse sworn
And the roaring boyes bravadoe.
The meeke, the white, the gentle,
Me handle touch and spare not
But those that crosse Tom Rynosseros
Doe what the panther dare not.

Although I sing, etc.

With an host of furious fancies,
Whereof I am commander,
With a burning speare, and a horse of aire,
To the wildernesse I wander.
By a knight of ghostes and shadowes
I summon'd am to tourney
Ten leagues beyond the wide world's end,
Me thinke it is noe journey.

Yet will I sing, etc.

JOHN DONNE

(1572–1601, British)

The Relic

When my grave is broke up again
Some second guest to entertain,
(For graves have learned that woman-head
To be to more than one a bed)
    And he that digs it, spies
A bracelet of bright hair about the bone,
    Will he not let us alone,
And think that there a loving couple lies,
Who thought that this device might be some way
To make their souls, at the last busy day,
Meet at this grave, and make a little stay?

If this fall in a time, or land,
Where mis-devotion doth command,
Then, he that digs us up, will bring
Us, to the Bishop, and the King,
    To make us relics; then
Thou shalt be a Mary Magdalen, and I   .
    A something else thereby;
All women shall adore us, and some men;
And since at such time, miracles are sought,
I would have that age by this paper taught
What miracles we harmless lovers wrought.

First, we loved well and faithfully,
Yet knew not what we loved, nor why,

Difference of sex no more we knew,
  Than our guardian angels do;
    Coming and going, we
Perchance might kiss, but not between those meals;
    Our hands ne'er touched the seals,
Which nature, injured by late law, sets free:
These miracles we did; but now alas,
All measure, and all language, I should pass,
Should I tell what a miracle she was.

BEN JONSON

(1572–1637, British)

*Epitaph on Salomon Pavy,
a Child of Queen Elizabeth's Chapel*

Weep with me, all you that read
   This little story;
And know for whom a tear you shed,
   Death's self is sorry.
'Twas a child that so did thrive
   In grace and feature,
As Heaven and Nature seemed to strive
   Which owned the creature.
Years he numbered scarce thirteen
   When Fates turned cruel,
Yet three filled zodiacs had he been
   The stage's jewel;
And did act (what now we moan)
   Old men so duly,
As, sooth, the Parcae thought him one,
   He played so truly.
So, by error, to his fate
   They all consented;
But, viewing him since (alas, too late),
   They have repented,
And have sought (to give new birth)
   In baths to steep him;
But, being so much too good for earth,
   Heaven vows to keep him.

ROBERT HERRICK

(1591–1674, British)

The Mad Maid's Song

Good morrow to the day so fair,
Good morrow, sir, to you,
Good morrow to mine own torn hair
Bedabbled with the dew.

Good morrow to this primrose too,
Good morrow to each maid
That will with flowers the tomb bestrew
Wherein my love is laid.

Ah, woe is me, woe, woe is me,
Alack and welladay!
For pity, sir, find out that bee
Which bore my love away.

I'll seek him in your bonnet brave,
I'll seek him in your eyes.
Nay, now I think they've made his grave
I' the bed of strawberries.

I'll seek him there. I know, ere this,
The cold cold earth doth shake him;
But I will go, or send a kiss
By you, sir, to awake him.

Pray, hurt him not. Though he be dead,
He knows well who do love him,
And who with green turfs rear his head,
And who do rudely move him.

He's soft and tender (pray take heed),
With bands of cowslips bind him
And bring him home; but 'tis decreed
That I shall never find him.

GEORGE HERBERT

(1593–1633, British)

———

Love bade me welcome:
yet my soul drew back

Love bade me welcome: yet my soul drew back,
      Guilty of dust and sin.
But quick-eyed Love, observing me grow slack
      From my first entrance in,
Drew nearer to me, sweetly questioning
      If I lacked anything.

"A guest," I answered, "worthy to be here":
      Love said, "You shall be he."
"I, the unkind, ungrateful? Ah, my dear,
      I cannot look on thee."
Love took my hand, and smiling did reply,
      "Who made the eyes but I?"

"Truth, Lord; but I have marred them; let my shame
      Go where it doth deserve."
"And know you not," says Love, "who bore the blame?"
      "My dear, then I will serve."
"You must sit down," says Love, "and taste my meat."
      So I did sit and eat.

THOMAS CAREW

(1594–1640, British)

———

A Song

Ask me no more where Jove bestows,
When June is past, the fading rose;
For in your beauties orient deep,
These flowers, as in their causes, sleep.

Ask me no more whither do stray
The golden atoms of the day;
For in pure love heaven did prepare
Those powders to enrich your hair.

Ask me no more whither doth haste
The nightingale when May is past;
For in your sweet dividing throat
She winters, and keeps warm her note.

Ask me no more where those stars light,
That downwards fall in dead of night;
For in your eyes they sit, and there
Fixèd become, as in their sphere.

Ask me no more if east or west
The phoenix builds her spicy nest;
For unto you at last she flies,
And in your fragrant bosom dies.

JAMES SHIRLEY

(1596–1666, British)

―――

Dirge

The glories of our blood and state
   Are shadows, not substantial things,
There is no armour against fate,
   Death lays his icy hand on Kings;
      Scepter and crown,
      Must tumble down,
And in the dust be equal made,
With the poor crooked scythe and spade.

Some men with swords may reap the field,
   And plant fresh laurels where they kill,
But their strong nerves at last must yield,
   They tame but one another still;
      Early or late,
      They stoop to fate,
And must give up the murmuring breath,
When they, pale captives, creep to death.

The garlands wither on your brow,
   Then boast no more your mighty deeds;
Upon death's purple altar now,
   See where the victor-victim bleeds,
      Your heads must come,
      To the cold tomb;
Only the actions of the just
Smell sweet, and blossom in their dust.

EDMUND WALLER

(1606–1687, British)

———

Of English Verse

Poets may boast, as safely vain,
Their work shall with the world remain;
Both bound together live or die,
The verses and the prophecy.

But who can hope his lines should long
Last in a daily changing tongue?
While they are new, envỳ prevails,
And as that dies, our language fails.

When architects have done their part,
The matter may betray their art;
Time, if we use ill-chosen stone,
Soon brings a well-built palace down.

Poets that lasting marble seek
Must carve in Latin or in Greek;
We write in sand, our language grows,
And like the tide our work o'erflows.

Chaucer his sense can only boast,
The glory of his numbers lost!
Years have defaced his matchless strain;
And yet he did not sing in vain.

The beauties which adorned that age,
The shining subjects of his rage,
Hoping they should immortal prove,
Rewarded with success his love.

This was the generous poet's scope,
And all an English pen can hope,
To make the fair approve his flame
That can so far extend their name.

Verse thus designed has no ill fate
If it arrive but at the date
Of fading beauty, if it prove
But as long-lived as present love.

WILLIAM DAVENANT

(1606–1668, British)

———

The Philosopher and the Lover;
To a Mistress Dying

Lover

Your Beauty, ripe, and calm, and fresh,
  As Eastern Summers are,
Must now, forsaking Time and Flesh,
  Add light to some small Star.

Philosopher

Whilst she yet lives, were Stars decay'd,
  Their light by hers, relief might find:
But Death will lead her to a shade
  Where Love is cold, and Beauty blinde.

Lover

Lovers (whose Priests all Poets are)
  Think ev'ry Mistress, when she dies,
Is chang'd at least into a Starr:
  And who dares doubt the Poets wise?

Philosopher

But ask not Bodies doom'd to die,
    To what abode they go;
Since Knowledge is but sorrows Spy,
    It is not safe to know.

JOHN MILTON

(1608–1674, British)

―――

*When I consider how my
light is spent*

When I consider how my light is spent
   Ere half my days, in this dark world and wide,
   And that one talent which is death to hide
   Lodged with me useless, though my soul more bent
To serve therewith my Maker, and present
   My true account, lest he returning chide;
   "Doth God exact day-labor, light denied?"
   I fondly ask; but Patience to prevent
That murmur, soon replies, "God doth not need
   Either man's work or his own gifts; who best
   Bear his mild yoke, they serve him best. His state
Is kingly. Thousands at his bidding speed
   And post o'er land and ocean without rest:
   They also serve who only stand and wait."

WILLIAM CARTWRIGHT

(1611–1643, British)

———

No Platonique Love

Tell me no more of Minds embracing Minds,
    And hearts exchang'd for hearts;
That Spirits Spirits meet, as Winds do winds,
    And mix their subt'lest parts;
That two unbodi'd Essences may kiss,
And then like Angels, twist and feel one Bliss.

I was that silly thing that once was wrought
    To Practise this thin Love;
I climb'd from Sex to Soul, from Soul to Thought;
    But thinking there to move,
Headlong I rowl'd from Thought to Soul, and then
From Soul I lighted at the Sex agen.

As some strict down-look'd Men pretend to fast,
    Who yet in Closets Eat;
So Lovers who profess they Spirits taste,
    Feed yet on grosser meat;
I know they boast they Soules to Souls Convey,
How e'er they meet, the Body is the Way.

Come, I will undeceive thee, they that tread
    Those vain Aëriall waies,
Are like young Heyrs, and Alchymists misled
    To waste their Wealth and Daies,
For searching thus to be for ever Rich,
They only find a Med'cine for the Itch.

[48]

ANDREW MARVELL

(1621–1678, British)

To His Coy Mistress

Had we but world enough, and time,
This coyness, Lady, were no crime.
We would sit down, and think which way
To walk, and pass our long love's day.
Thou by the Indian Ganges' side
Shouldst rubies find: I by the tide
Of Humber would complain. I would
Love you ten years before the flood:
And you should, if you please, refuse
Till the conversion of the Jews.
My vegetable love should grow
Vaster than empires, and more slow.
An hundred years should go to praise
Thine eyes, and on thy forehead gaze.
Two hundred to adore each breast:
But thirty thousand to the rest.
An age at least to every part,
And the last age should show your heart:
For, Lady, you deserve this state;
Nor would I love at lower rate.
    But at my back I always hear
Time's wingèd chariot hurrying near:
And yonder all before us lie
Deserts of vast eternity.
Thy beauty shall no more be found;
Nor, in thy marble vault, shall sound

My echoing song: then worms shall try
That long-preserved virginity:
And your quaint honour turn to dust;
And into ashes all my lust.
The grave's a fine and private place,
But none, I think, do there embrace.
   Now, therefore, while the youthful hue
Sits on thy skin like morning dew,
And while thy willing soul transpires
At every pore with instant fires,
Now let us sport us while we may;
And now, like amorous birds of prey,
Rather at once our time devour,
Than languish in his slow-chapped power.
Let us roll all our strength, and all
Our sweetness, up into one ball:
And tear our pleasures with rough strife,
Through the iron gates of life.
Thus, though we cannot make our sun
Stand still, yet we will make him run.

HENRY VAUGHAN

(1621–1695, British)

———

Corruption

Sure it was so. Man in those early days
   Was not all stone and earth;
He shined a little, and by those weak rays
   Had some glimpse of his birth.
He saw heaven o'er his head, and knew from whence
   He came, condemnèd, hither;
And, as first love draws strongest, so from hence
   His mind sure progressed thither.
Things here were strange unto him: sweat and till,
   All was a thorn or weed:
Nor did those last, but (like himself) died still
   As soon as they did seed.
They seemed to quarrel with him, for that act
   That felled him foiled them all:
He drew the curse upon the world, and cracked
   The whole frame with his fall.
This made him long for home, as loath to stay
   With murmurers and foes;
He sighed for Eden, and would often say,
   "Ah! what bright days were those!"
Nor was heaven cold unto him; for each day
   The valley or the mountain
Afforded visits, and still Paradise lay
   In some green shade or fountain.
Angels lay lieger here; each bush and cell,
   Each oak and highway knew them;

Walk but the fields, or sit down at some well,
    And he was sure to view them.
Almighty Love! where art thou now? Mad man
    Sits down and freezeth on;
He raves, and swears to stir nor fire, nor fan,
    But bids the thread be spun.
I see, thy curtains are close-drawn; thy bow
    Looks dim, too, in the cloud;
Sin triumphs still, and man is sunk below
    The center, and his shroud.
All's in deep sleep and night: thick darkness lies
    And hatcheth o'er thy people —
But hark! what trumpet's that? what angel cries,
    "Arise! thrust in thy sickle"?

MARGARET CAVENDISH
Duchess of Newcastle
(1623–1673, British)

———

A Discourse of Melancholy

A sad and solemn verse doth please the mind,
With chains of passions doth the spirits bind.
As pencilled pictures drawn presents the night,
Whose darker shadows give the eye delight,
Melancholy aspects invite the eye,
And always have a seeming majesty.
By its converting qualities there grows
A perfect likeness, when itself it shows.
Then let the world in mourning sit and weep,
Since only sadness we are apt to keep.
In light and toyish things we seek for change;
The mind grows weary, and about doth range.
What serious is, there constancies will dwell;
Which shows that sadness mirth doth far excel.
Why should men grieve when they do think of death,
Since they no settlement can have in mirth?
The grave, though sad, in quiet still they keep:
Without disturbing dreams they lie asleep,
No rambling thoughts to vex their restless brains,
Nor labour hard, to scorch and dry their veins.
No care to search for that they cannot find,
Which is an appetite to every mind.
Then wish, good man, to die in quiet peace,
Since death in misery is a release.

MARY, LADY CHUDLEIGH

(1656–1710, British)

———

To the Ladies

Wife and servant are the same,
But only differ in the name:
For when that fatal knot is tied,
Which nothing, nothing can divide,
When she the word *Obey* has said,
And man by law supreme has made,
Then all that's kind is laid aside,
And nothing left but state and pride.
Fierce as an eastern prince he grows,
And all his innate rigour shows:
Then but to look, to laugh, or speak,
Will the nuptial contract break.
Like mutes, she signs alone must make,
And never any freedom take,
But still be governed by a nod,
And fear her husband as her god:
Him still must serve, him still obey,
And nothing act, and nothing say,
But what her haughty lord thinks fit,
Who, with the power, has all the wit.
Then shun, oh! shun that wretched state,
And all the fawning flatterers hate.
Value yourselves, and men despise:
You must be proud, if you'll be wise.

ANNE FINCH
Countess of Winchilsea
(1661–1720, British)

———

A Nocturnal Reverie

In such a night, when every louder wind
Is to its distant cavern safe confined;
And only gentle Zephyr fans his wings,
And lonely Philomel, still waking, sings;
Or from some tree, famed for the owl's delight,
She, hollowing clear, directs the wanderer right:
In such a night, when passing clouds give place,
Or thinly veil the heavens' mysterious face;
When in some river, overhung with green,
The waving moon and trembling leaves are seen;
When freshened grass now bears itself upright,
And makes cool banks to pleasing rest invite,
Whence springs the woodbind, and the bramble-rose,
And where the sleepy cowslip sheltered grows;
Whilst now a paler hue the foxglove takes,
Yet checkers still with red the dusky brakes:
When scattered glow-worms, but in twilight fine,
Show trivial beauties watch their hour to shine;
Whilst Salisbury stands the test of every light,
In perfect charms, and perfect virtue bright:
When odors, which declined repelling day,
Through temperate air uninterrupted stray;
When darkened groves their softest shadows wear,
And falling waters we distinctly hear;
When through the gloom more venerable shows

Some ancient fabric, awful in repose,
While sunburnt hills their swarthy looks conceal,
And swelling haycocks thicken up the vale:
When the loosed horse now, as his pasture leads,
Comes slowly grazing through the adjoining meads,
Whose stealing pace, and lengthened shade we fear,
Till torn-up forage in his teeth we hear:
When nibbling sheep at large pursue their food,
And unmolested kine rechew the cud;
When curlews cry beneath the village walls,
And to her straggling brood the partridge calls;
Their shortlived jubilee the creatures keep,
Which but endures, whilst tyrant man does sleep;
When a sedate content the spirit feels,
And no fierce light disturbs, whilst it reveals;
But silent musings urge the mind to seek
Something, too high for syllables to speak;
Till the free soul to a composedness charmed,
Finding the elements of rage disarmed,
O'er all below a solemn quiet grown,
Joys in the inferior world, and thinks it like her own:
In such a night let me abroad remain,
Till morning breaks, and all's confused again;
Our cares, our toils, our clamors are renewed,
Or pleasures, seldom reached, again pursued.

JONATHAN SWIFT

(1667–1745, British)

———

The Progress of Beauty

When first Diana leaves her Bed
Vapors and Steams her Looks disgrace,
A frouzy dirty colour'd red
Sits on her cloudy wrinckled Face.

But by degrees when mounted high
Her artificiall Face appears
Down from her Window in the Sky,
Her Spots are gone, her Visage clears.

'Twixt earthly Femals and the Moon
All Parallells exactly run;
If Celia should appear too soon
Alas, the Nymph would be undone.

To see her from her Pillow rise
All reeking in a cloudy Steam,
Crackt Lips, foul Teeth, and gummy Eyes,
Poor Strephon, how would he blaspheme!

The Soot or Powder which was wont
To make her Hair look black as Jet,
Falls from her Tresses on her Front
A mingled Mass of Dirt and Sweat.

[57]

Three Colours, Black, and Red, and White,
So gracefull in their proper Place,
Remove them to a diff'rent Light
They form a frightfull hideous Face,

For instance; when the Lilly slipps
Into the Precincts of the Rose,
And takes Possession of the Lips,
Leaving the Purple to the Nose.

So Celia went entire to bed,
All her Complexions safe and sound,
But when she rose, the black and red
Though still in Sight, had chang'd their Ground.

The Black, which would not be confin'd
A more inferior Station seeks
Leaving the fiery red behind,
And mingles in her muddy Cheeks.

The Paint by Perspiration cracks,
And falls in Rivulets of Sweat,
On either Side you see the Tracks,
While at her Chin the Conflu'ents met.

A Skillfull Houswife thus her Thumb
With Spittle while she spins, anoints,
And thus the brown Meanders come
In trickling Streams betwixt her Joynts.

But Celia can with ease reduce
By help of Pencil, Paint and Brush
Each Colour to it's Place and Use,
And teach her Cheeks again to blush.

She knows her Early self no more,
But fill'd with Admiration, stands,
As Other Painters oft adore
The Workmanship of their own Hands.

Thus after four important Hours
Celia's the Wonder of her Sex;
Say, which among the Heav'nly Pow'rs
Could cause such wonderfull Effects.

Venus, indulgent to her Kind
Gave Women all their Hearts could wish
When first she taught them where to find
White Lead, and Lusitanian Dish.

Love with White lead cements his Wings,
White lead was sent us to repair
Two brightest, brittlest earthly Things
A Lady's Face, and China ware.

She ventures now to lift the Sash,
The Window is her proper Sphear;
Ah Lovely Nymph be not too rash,
Nor let the Beaux approach too near.

Take Pattern by your Sister Star,
Delude at once and Bless our Sight,
When you are seen, be seen from far,
And chiefly chuse to shine by Night.

In the Pell-mell when passing by,
Keep up the Glasses of your Chair,
Then each transported Fop will cry,
G—d d—m me Jack, she's wondrous fair.

[59]

But, Art no longer can prevayl
When the Materialls all are gone,
The best Mechanick Hand must fayl
Where Nothing's left to work upon.

Matter, as wise Logicians say,
Cannot without a Form subsist,
And Form, say I, as well as They,
Must fayl if Matter brings no Grist.

And this is fair Diana's Case
For, all Astrologers maintain
Each Night a Bit drops off her Face
When Mortals say she's in her Wain.

While Partridge wisely shews the Cause
Efficient of the Moon's Decay,
That Cancer with his pois'nous Claws
Attacks her in the milky Way:

But Gadbury in Art profound
From her pale Cheeks pretends to show
That Swain Endymion is not sound,
Or else, that Mercury's her Foe.

But, let the Cause be what it will,
In half a Month she looks so thin
That Flamstead can with all his Skill
See but her Forehead and her Chin.

Yet as she wasts, she grows discreet,
Till Midnight never shows her Head;
So rotting Celia stroles the Street
When sober Folks are all a-bed.

For sure if this be Luna's Fate,
Poor Celia, but of mortall Race
In vain expects a longer Date
To the Materialls of Her Face.

When Mercury her Tresses mows
To think of Oyl and Soot, is vain,
No Painting can restore a Nose,
Nor will her Teeth return again.

Two Balls of Glass may serve for Eyes,
White Lead can plaister up a Cleft,
But these alas, are poor Supplyes
If neither Cheeks, nor Lips be left.

Ye Pow'rs who over Love preside,
Since mortal Beautyes drop so soon,
If you would have us well supply'd,
Send us new Nymphs with each new Moon.

ALEXANDER POPE

(1688–1744, British)

———

Ode on Solitude

Happy the man whose wish and care
   A few paternal acres bound,
Content to breathe his native air,
         In his own ground.

Whose herds with milk, whose fields with bread,
   Whose flocks supply him with attire,
Whose trees in summer yield him shade,
         In winter fire.

Blest, who can unconcernedly find
   Hours, days, and years slide soft away,
In health of body, peace of mind,
         Quiet by day,

Sound sleep by night; study and ease,
   Together mixed; sweet recreation;
And innocence, which most does please
         With meditation.

Thus let me live, unseen, unknown;
   Thus unlamented let me die;
Steal from the world, and not a stone
         Tell where I lie.

WILLIAM BLAKE

(1757–1827, British)

The Sick Rose

O rose, thou art sick!
The invisible worm
That flies in the night,
In the howling storm,

Has found out thy bed
Of crimson joy,
And his dark secret love
Does thy life destroy.

ROBERT BURNS

(1759–1796, British)

To a Mouse

ON TURNING HER UP IN HER NEST
WITH THE PLOUGH, NOVEMBER, 1785

I

Wee, sleekit, cowrin, tim'rous beastie,
O, what a panic's in thy breastie!
Thou need na start awa sae hasty
                   Wi' bickering brattle!
I wad be laith to rin an' chase thee,
                   Wi' murdering pattle!

II

I'm truly sorry man's dominion
Has broken Nature's social union,
An' justifies that ill opinion
                   Which makes thee startle
At me, thy poor, earth-born companion
                   An' fellow mortal!

III

I doubt na, whyles, but thou may thieve;
What then? poor beastie, thou maun live
A daimen icker in a thrave

'S a sma' request;
I'll get a blessin wi' the lave,
　　　　　　An' never miss 't!

IV

Thy wee-bit housie, too, in ruin!
Its silly wa's the win's are strewin!
An' naething, now, to big a new ane,
　　　　　　O' foggage green!
An' bleak December's win's ensuin,
　　　　　　Baith snell an' keen!

V

Thou saw the fields laid bare an' waste,
An' weary winter comin fast,
An' cozie here, beneath the blast,
　　　　　　Thou thought to dwell,
Till crash! the cruel coulter past
　　　　　　Out thro' thy cell.

VI

That wee bit heap o' leaves an' stibble,
Has cost thee monie a weary nibble!
Now thou's turned out, for a' thy trouble,
　　　　　　But house or hald,
To thole the winter's sleety dribble,
　　　　　　An' cranreuch cauld!

VII

But Mousie, thou art no thy lane,
In proving foresight may be vain:

The best-laid schemes o' mice an' men
        Gang aft agley,
An' lea'e us nought but grief an' pain,
        For promis'd joy!

VIII

Still thou art blest, compared wi' me!
The present only toucheth thee:
But och! I backward cast my e'e,
        On prospects drear!
An' forward, tho' I canna see,
        I guess an' fear!

WILLIAM WORDSWORTH

(1770–1850, British)

———

Lucy Gray

Oft I had heard of Lucy Gray:
And, when I crossed the wild,
I chanced to see at break of day
The solitary child.

No mate, no comrade Lucy knew;
She dwelt on a wide moor,
– The sweetest thing that ever grew
Beside a human door!

You yet may spy the fawn at play,
The hare upon the green;
But the sweet face of Lucy Gray
Will never more be seen.

'Tonight will be a stormy night –
You to the town must go;
And take a lantern, Child, to light
Your mother through the snow.'

'That, Father! will I gladly do:
'Tis scarcely afternoon –
The minister-clock has just struck two,
And yonder is the moon!'

At this the Father raised his hook,
And snapped a faggot-band;
He plied his work; — and Lucy took
The lantern in her hand.

Not blither is the mountain roe:
With many a wanton stroke
Her feet disperse the powdery snow,
That rises up like smoke.

The storm came on before its time:
She wandered up and down;
And many a hill did Lucy climb:
But never reached the town.

The wretched parents all that night
Went shouting far and wide;
But there was neither sound nor sight
To serve them for a guide.

At day-break on a hill they stood
That overlooked the moor;
And thence they saw the bridge of wood,
A furlong from their door.

They wept — and, turning homeward, cried,
'In heaven we all shall meet';
— When in the snow the mother spied
The print of Lucy's feet.

Then downwards from the steep hill's edge
They tracked the footmarks small;
And through the broken hawthorn hedge,
And by the long stone-wall;

And then an open field they crossed:
The marks were still the same;
They tracked them on, nor ever lost;
And to the bridge they came.

They followed from the snowy bank
Those footmarks, one by one,
Into the middle of the plank;
And further there were none!

—Yet some maintain that to this day
She is a living child;
That you may see sweet Lucy Gray
Upon the lonesome wild.

O'er rough and smooth she trips along,
And never looks behind;
And sings a solitary song
That whistles in the wind.

WALTER SCOTT

(1771–1832, British)

———

Proud Maisie

Proud Maisie is in the wood,
   Walking so early;
Sweet Robin sits on the bush,
   Singing so rarely.

"Tell me, thou bonny bird,
   When shall I marry me?"
"When six braw gentlemen,
   Kirkward shall carry ye."

"Who makes the bridal bed,
   Birdie, say truly?" —
"The gray-headed sexton
   That delves the grave duly.

"The glow-worm o'er grave and stone
   Shall light thee steady;
The owl from the steeple sing,
   'Welcome, proud lady.'"

SAMUEL TAYLOR COLERIDGE

(1772–1834, British)

———

Kubla Khan

In Xanadu did Kubla Khan
A stately pleasure-dome decree:
Where Alph, the sacred river, ran
Through caverns measureless to man
   Down to a sunless sea.
So twice five miles of fertile ground
With walls and towers were girdled round:
And there were gardens bright with sinuous rills,
Where blossomed many an incense-bearing tree;
And here were forests ancient as the hills,
Enfolding sunny spots of greenery.

But oh! that deep romantic chasm which slanted
Down the green hill athwart a cedarn cover!
A savage place! as holy and enchanted
As e'er beneath a waning moon was haunted
By woman wailing for her demon-lover!
And from this chasm, with ceaseless turmoil seething,
As if this earth in fast thick pants were breathing,
A mighty fountain momently was forced:
Amid whose swift half-intermitted burst
Huge fragments vaulted like rebounding hail,
Or chaffy grain beneath the thresher's flail:
And 'mid these dancing rocks at once and ever
It flung up momently the sacred river.
Five miles meandering with a mazy motion

Through wood and dale the sacred river ran,
Then reached the caverns measureless to man,
And sank in tumult to a lifeless ocean:
And 'mid this tumult Kubla heard from far
Ancestral voices prophesying war!
　　The shadow of the dome of pleasure
　　Floated midway on the waves;
　　Where was heard the mingled measure
　　From the fountain and the caves.
It was a miracle of rare device,
A sunny pleasure-dome with caves of ice!

　　A damsel with a dulcimer
　　In a vision once I saw:
　　It was an Abyssinian maid,
　　And on her dulcimer she played,
　　Singing of Mount Abora.
　　Could I revive within me
　　Her symphony and song,
　　To such a deep delight 'twould win me,
That with music loud and long,
I would build that dome in air,
That sunny dome! those caves of ice!
And all who heard should see them there,
And all should cry, Beware! Beware!
His flashing eyes, his floating hair!
Weave a circle round him thrice,
And close your eyes with holy dread,
For he on honey-dew hath fed,
And drunk the milk of Paradise.

GEORGE GORDON, LORD BYRON

(1788–1824, British)

———

Darkness

I had a dream, which was not all a dream.
The bright sun was extinguished, and the stars
Did wander darkling in the eternal space,
Rayless, and pathless, and the icy Earth
Swung blind and blackening in the moonless air;
Morn came and went — and came, and brought no day,
And men forgot their passions in the dread
Of this their desolation; and all hearts
Were chilled into a selfish prayer for light:
And they did live by watchfires — and the thrones,
The palaces of crownéd kings — the huts,
The habitations of all things which dwell,
Were burnt for beacons; cities were consumed,
And men were gathered round their blazing homes
To look once more into each other's face;
Happy were those who dwelt within the eye
Of the volcanos, and their mountain-torch:
A fearful hope was all the world contained;
Forests were set on fire — but hour by hour
They fell and faded — and the crackling trunks
Extinguished with a crash — and all was black.
The brows of men by the despairing light
Wore an unearthly aspect, as by fits
The flashes fell upon them; some lay down
And hid their eyes and wept; and some did rest
Their chins upon their clenchéd hands, and smiled;

And others hurried to and fro, and fed
Their funeral piles with fuel, and looked up
With mad disquietude on the dull sky,
The pall of a past World; and then again
With curses cast them down upon the dust,
And gnashed their teeth and howled: the wild birds
   shrieked,
And, terrified, did flutter on the ground,
And flap their useless wings; the wildest brutes
Came tame and tremulous; and vipers crawled
And twined themselves among the multitude,
Hissing, but stingless — they were slain for food:
And War, which for a moment was no more,
Did glut himself again: — a meal was bought
With blood, and each sate sullenly apart
Gorging himself in gloom: no Love was left;
All earth was but one thought — and that was Death,
Immediate and inglorious; and the pang
Of famine fed upon all entrails — men
Died, and their bones were tombless as their flesh;
The meagre by the meagre were devoured,
Even dogs assailed their masters, all save one,
And he was faithful to a corse, and kept
The birds and beasts and famished men at bay,
Till hunger clung them, or the dropping dead
Lured their lank jaws; himself sought out no food,
But with a piteous and perpetual moan,
And a quick desolate cry, licking the hand
Which answered not with a caress — he died.
The crowd was famished by degrees; but two
Of an enormous city did survive,
And they were enemies: they met beside
The dying embers of an altar-place
Where had been heaped a mass of holy things
For an unholy usage; they raked up,

And shivering scraped with their cold skeleton hands
The feeble ashes, and their feeble breath
Blew for a little life, and made a flame
Which was a mockery; then they lifted up
Their eyes as it grew lighter, and beheld
Each other's aspects — saw, and shrieked, and died —
Even of their mutual hideousness they died,
Unknowing who he was upon whose brow
Famine had written Fiend. The World was void,
The populous and the powerful was a lump,
Seasonless, herbless, treeless, manless, lifeless —
A lump of death — a chaos of hard clay.
The rivers, lakes, and ocean all stood still,
And nothing stirred within their silent depths;
Ships sailorless lay rotting on the sea,
And their masts fell down piecemeal: as they dropped
They slept on the abyss without a surge —
The waves were dead; the tides were in their grave,
The Moon, their mistress, had expired before;
The winds were withered in the stagnant air,
And the clouds perished; Darkness had no need
Of aid from them — She was the Universe.

PERCY BYSSHE SHELLEY

(1792–1822, British)

———

When the lamp is shattered

I

When the lamp is shattered,
The light in the dust lies dead—
　When the cloud is scattered,
The rainbow's glory is shed.
　When the lute is broken,
Sweet tones are remembered not;
　When the lips have spoken,
Loved accents are soon forgot.

II

　As music and splendour
Survive not the lamp and the lute,
　The heart's echoes render
No song when the spirit is mute:—
　No song but sad dirges,
Like the wind through a ruined cell,
　Or the mournful surges
That ring the dead seaman's knell.

III

　When hearts have once mingled,
Love first leaves the well-built nest;

The weak one is singled
To endure what it once possesst.
O, Love! who bewailest
The frailty of all things here,
Why choose you the frailest
For your cradle, your home, and your bier?

IV

Its passions will rock thee,
As the storms rock the ravens on high;
Bright reason will mock thee,
Like the sun from a wintry sky.
From thy nest every rafter
Will rot, and thine eagle home
Leave thee naked to laughter,
When leaves fall and cold winds come.

JOHN CLARE

(1793–1864, British)

———

The Badger

The badger grunting on his woodland track
With shaggy hide and sharp nose scrowed with black
Roots in the bushes and the woods and makes
A great huge burrow in the ferns and brakes
With nose on ground he runs an awkward pace
And anything will beat him in the race
The shepherd's dog will run him to his den
Followed and hooted by the dogs and men
The woodman when the hunting comes about
Go round at night to stop the foxes out
And hurrying through the bushes ferns and brakes
Nor sees the many holes the badger makes
And often through the bushes to the chin
Breaks the old holes and tumbles headlong in

When midnight comes a host of dogs and men
Go out and track the badger to his den
And put a sack within the hole and lie
Till the old grunting badger passes by
He comes and hears they let the strongest loose
The old fox hears the noise and drops the goose
The poacher shoots and hurries from the cry
And the old hare half wounded buzzes by.
They get a forkèd stick to bear him down
And clap the dogs and take him to the town
And bait him all the day with many dogs

And laugh and shout and fright the scampering hogs
He runs along and bites at all he meets;
They shout and hollo down the noisy streets

He turns about to face the loud uproar
And drives the rebels to their very doors
The frequent stone is hurled where'ere they go
When badgers fight, then everyone's a foe
The dogs are clapt and urged to join the fray
The badger turns and drives them all away
Though scarcely half as big, dimute and small
He fights with dogs for hours and beats them all
The heavy mastiff savage in the fray
Lies down and licks his feet and turns away
The bulldog knows his match and waxes cold
The badger grins and never leaves his hold
He drives the crowd and follows at their heels
And bites them through – the drunkard swears and reels

The frightened women take the boys away
The blackguard laughs and hurries on the fray
He tries to reach the woods an awkward race
But sticks and cudgels quickly stop the chase
He turns again and drives the noisy crowd
And beats the many dogs in noises loud
He drives away and beats them every one
And then they loose them all and set them on
He falls as dead and kicked by boys and men
Then starts and grins and drives the crowd again
Till kicked and torn and beaten out he lies
And leaves his hold and cackles, groans and dies.

WILLIAM CULLEN BRYANT

(1794–1878, American)

———

To Cole, the Painter,
Departing for Europe

Thine eyes shall see the light of distant skies;
    Yet, Cole! thy heart shall bear to Europe's strand
    A living image of our own bright land,
Such as upon thy glorious canvas lies;
Lone lakes — savannas where the bison roves —
    Rocks rich with summer garlands — solemn streams —
    Skies, where the desert eagle wheels and screams —
Spring bloom and autumn blaze of boundless groves.
Fair scenes shall greet thee where thou goest — fair,
    But different — everywhere the trace of men,
    Paths, homes, graves, ruins, from the lowest glen
To where life shrinks from the fierce Alpine air —
    Gaze on them, till the tears shall dim thy sight,
    But keep that earlier, wilder image bright.

JOHN KEATS

(1795–1821, British)

———

Ode to a Nightingale

1

My heart aches, and a drowsy numbness pains
  My sense, as though of hemlock I had drunk,
Or emptied some dull opiate to the drains
  One minute past, and Lethe-wards had sunk:
'Tis not through envy of thy happy lot,
  But being too happy in thine happiness, —
    That thou, light-winged Dryad of the trees,
      In some melodious plot
Of beechen green, and shadows numberless,
  Singest of summer in full-throated ease.

2

O for a draught of vintage! that hath been
  Cool'd a long age in the deep-delved earth,
Tasting of Flora and the country green,
  Dance, and Provençal song, and sunburnt mirth!
O for a beaker full of the warm South,
  Full of the true, the blushful Hippocrene,
    With beaded bubbles winking at the brim,
      And purple-stained mouth;
That I might drink, and leave the world unseen,
  And with thee fade away into the forest dim:

3

Fade far away, dissolve, and quite forget
    What thou among the leaves hast never known,
The weariness, the fever, and the fret
    Here, where men sit and hear each other groan;
Where palsy shakes a few, sad, last grey hairs,
        Where youth grows pale, and spectre-thin, and dies;
            Where but to think is to be full of sorrow
                And leaden-eyed despairs,
        Where Beauty cannot keep her lustrous eyes,
            Or new Love pine at them beyond to-morrow.

4

Away! away! for I will fly to thee,
    Not charioted by Bacchus and his pards,
But on the viewless wings of Poesy,
    Though the dull brain perplexes and retards:
Already with thee! tender is the night,
        And haply the Queen-Moon is on her throne,
            Cluster'd around by all her starry Fays;
                But here there is no light,
        Save what from heaven is with the breezes blown
            Through verdurous glooms and winding mossy ways.

5

I cannot see what flowers are at my feet,
    Nor what soft incense hangs upon the boughs,
But, in embalmed darkness, guess each sweet
    Wherewith the seasonable month endows
The grass, the thicket, and the fruit-tree wild;
    White hawthorn, and the pastoral eglantine;
        Fast fading violets cover'd up in leaves;

And mid-May's eldest child,
The coming musk-rose, full of dewy wine,
    The murmurous haunt of flies on summer eves.

6

Darkling I listen; and, for many a time
    I have been half in love with easeful Death,
Call'd him soft names in many a mused rhyme,
    To take into the air my quiet breath;
Now more than ever seems it rich to die,
    To cease upon the midnight with no pain,
        While thou art pouring forth thy soul abroad
            In such an ecstasy!
    Still wouldst thou sing, and I have ears in vain —
        To thy high requiem become a sod.

7

Thou wast not born for death, immortal Bird!
    No hungry generations tread thee down;
The voice I hear this passing night was heard
    In ancient days by emperor and clown:
Perhaps the self-same song that found a path
    Through the sad heart of Ruth, when, sick for home,
        She stood in tears amid the alien corn;
            The same that oft-times hath
    Charm'd magic casements, opening on the foam
        Of perilous seas, in faery lands forlorn.

8

Forlorn! the very word is like a bell
    To toll me back from thee to my sole self!
Adieu! the fancy cannot cheat so well

As she is fam'd to do, deceiving elf.
Adieu! adieu! thy plaintive anthem fades
Past the near meadows, over the still stream,
Up the hill-side; and now 'tis buried deep
In the next valley-glades:
Was it a vision, or a waking dream?
Fled is that music: — Do I wake or sleep?

RALPH WALDO EMERSON

(1803–1882, American)

―――

The Rhodora

In May, when sea-winds pierced our solitudes,
I found the fresh Rhodora in the woods,
Spreading its leafless blooms in a damp nook,
To please the desert and the sluggish brook.
The purple petals, fallen in the pool,
Made the black water with their beauty gay;
Here might the red-bird come his plumes to cool,
And court the flower that cheapens his array.
Rhodora! if the sages ask thee why
This charm is wasted on the earth and sky,
Tell them, dear, that if eyes were made for seeing,
Then Beauty is its own excuse for being:
Why thou wert there, O rival of the rose!
I never thought to ask, I never knew:
But, in my simple ignorance, suppose
The self-same Power that brought me there brought you.

HENRY WADSWORTH LONGFELLOW

(1807–1882, American)

———

Snow-Flakes

Out of the bosom of the Air,
  Out of the cloud-folds of her garments shaken,
Over the woodlands brown and bare,
  Over the harvest-fields forsaken,
    Silent, and soft, and slow
    Descends the snow.

Even as our cloudy fancies take
  Suddenly shape in some divine expression,
Even as the troubled heart doth make
  In the white countenance confession,
    The troubled sky reveals
    The grief it feels.

This is the poem of the air,
  Slowly in silent syllables recorded;
This is the secret of despair,
  Long in its cloudy bosom hoarded,
    Now whispered and revealed
    To wood and field.

JOHN GREENLEAF WHITTIER

(1807–1892, American)

———

Telling the Bees

Here is the place; right over the hill
   Runs the path I took;
You can see the gap in the old wall still,
   And the stepping-stones in the shallow brook.

There is the house, with the gate red-barred,
   And the poplars tall;
And the barn's brown length, and the cattle-yard,
   And the white horns tossing above the wall.

There are the beehives ranged in the sun;
   And down by the brink
Of the brook are her poor flowers, weed-o'errun,
   Pansy and daffodil, rose and pink.

A year has gone, as the tortoise goes,
   Heavy and slow;
And the same rose blows, and the same sun glows,
   And the same brook sings of a year ago.

There's the same sweet clover-smell in the breeze;
   And the June sun warm
Tangles his wings of fire in the trees,
   Setting, as then, over Fernside farm.

I mind me how with a lover's care
　　From my Sunday coat
I brushed off the burrs, and smoothed my hair,
　　And cooled at the brookside my brow and throat.

Since we parted, a month had passed, —
　　To love, a year;
Down through the beeches I looked at last
　　On the little red gate and the well-sweep near.

I can see it all now, — the slantwise rain
　　Of light through the leaves,
The sundown's blaze on her window-pane,
　　The bloom of her roses under the eaves.

Just the same as a month before, —
　　The house and the trees,
The barn's brown gable, the vine by the door, —
　　Nothing changed but the hives of bees.

Before them, under the garden wall,
　　Forward and back,
Went drearily singing the chore-girl small,
　　Draping each hive with a shred of black.

Trembling, I listened: the summer sun
　　Had the chill of snow;
For I knew she was telling the bees of one
　　Gone on the journey we all must go!

Then I said to myself, "My Mary weeps
　　For the dead to-day:
Haply her blind old grandsire sleeps
　　The fret and the pain of his age away."

But her dog whined low; on the doorway sill,
    With his cane to his chin,
The old man sat; and the chore-girl still
    Sang to the bees stealing out and in.

And the song she was singing ever since
    In my ear sounds on: —
"Stay at home, pretty bees, fly not hence!
    Mistress Mary is dead and gone!"

EDGAR ALLAN POE

(1809–1849, American)

―――

Annabel Lee

It was many and many a year ago,
   In a kingdom by the sea,
That a maiden there lived whom you may know
   By the name of Annabel Lee; –
And this maiden she lived with no other thought
   Than to love and be loved by me.

I was a child and *she* was a child,
   In this kingdom by the sea;
But we loved with a love that was more than love –
   I and my Annabel Lee –
With a love that the wingéd seraphs in Heaven
   Coveted her and me.

And this was the reason that, long ago,
   In this kingdom by the sea,
A wind blew out of a cloud, chilling
   My beautiful Annabel Lee;
So that her high-born kinsmen came
   And bore her away from me,
To shut her up in a sepulchre,
   In this kingdom by the sea.

The angels, not half so happy in Heaven,
   Went envying her and me –
Yes! – that was the reason (as all men know,

In this kingdom by the sea)
That the wind came out of the cloud by night,
    Chilling and killing my Annabel Lee.

But our love it was stronger by far than the love
    Of those who were older than we —
    Of many far wiser than we —
And neither the angels in Heaven above,
    Nor the demons down under the sea,
Can ever dissever my soul from the soul
    Of the beautiful Annabel Lee: —

For the moon never beams, without bringing me dreams
    Of the beautiful Annabel Lee;
And the stars never rise, but I feel the bright eyes
    Of the beautiful Annabel Lee: —
And so, all the night-tide, I lie down by the side
Of my darling — my darling — my life and my bride,
    In her sepulchre there by the sea —
    In her tomb by the sounding sea.

ALFRED, LORD TENNYSON

(1809–1892, British)

Tithonus

The woods decay, the woods decay and fall,
The vapors weep their burthen to the ground,
Man comes and tills the field and lies beneath,
And after many a summer dies the swan.
Me only cruel immortality
Consumes; I wither slowly in thine arms,
Here at the quiet limit of the world,
A white-haired shadow roaming like a dream
The ever-silent spaces of the East,
Far-folded mists, and gleaming halls of morn.
    Alas! for this gray shadow, once a man —
So glorious in his beauty and thy choice,
Who madest him thy chosen, that he seemed
To his great heart none other than a God!
I asked thee, "Give me immortality."
Then didst thou grant mine asking with a smile,
Like wealthy men who care not how they give.
But thy strong Hours indignant worked their wills,
And beat me down and marred and wasted me,
And though they could not end me, left me maimed
To dwell in presence of immortal youth,
Immortal age beside immortal youth,
And all I was in ashes. Can thy love,
Thy beauty, make amends, though even now,
Close over us, the silver star, thy guide,
Shines in those tremulous eyes that fill with tears

To hear me? Let me go; take back thy gift.
Why should a man desire in any way
To vary from the kindly race of men,
Or pass beyond the goal of ordinance
Where all should pause, as is most meet for all?

A soft air fans the cloud apart; there comes
A glimpse of that dark world where I was born.
Once more the old mysterious glimmer steals
From thy pure brows, and from thy shoulders pure,
And bosom beating with a heart renewed.
Thy cheek begins to redden through the gloom,
Thy sweet eyes brighten slowly close to mine,
Ere yet they blind the stars, and the wild team
Which love thee, yearning for thy yoke, arise,
And shake the darkness from their loosened manes,
And beat the twilight into flakes of fire.

Lo! ever thus thou growest beautiful
In silence, then before thine answer given
Departest, and thy tears are on my cheek.

Why wilt thou ever scare me with thy tears,
And make me tremble lest a saying learnt,
In days far-off, on that dark earth, be true?
"The Gods themselves cannot recall their gifts."

Ay me! ay me! with what another heart
In days far-off, and with what other eyes
I used to watch — if I be he that watched —
The lucid outline forming round thee; saw
The dim curls kindle into sunny rings;
Changed with thy mystic change, and felt my blood
Glow with the glow that slowly crimsoned all
Thy presence and thy portals, while I lay,
Mouth, forehead, eyelids, growing dewy-warm
With kisses balmier than half-opening buds
Of April, and could hear the lips that kissed
Whispering I knew not what of wild and sweet,

Like that strange song I heard Apollo sing,
While Ilion like a mist rose into towers.
    Yet hold me not forever in thine East;
How can my nature longer mix with thine?
Coldly thy rosy shadows bathe me, cold
Are all thy lights, and cold my wrinkled feet
Upon thy glimmering thresholds, when the steam
Floats up from those dim fields about the homes
Of happy men that have the power to die,
And grassy barrows of the happier dead.
Release me, and restore me to the ground.
Thou seest all things, thou wilt see my grave;
Thou wilt renew thy beauty morn by morn,
I earth in earth forget these empty courts,
And thee returning on thy silver wheels.

ROBERT BROWNING

(1812–1889, British)

———

Memorabilia

I

Ah, did you once see Shelley plain,
 And did he stop and speak to you
And did you speak to him again?
 How strange it seems and new!

II

But you were living before that,
 And also you are living after;
And the memory I started at —
 My starting moves your laughter.

III

I crossed a moor, with a name of its own
 And a certain use in the world no doubt,
Yet a hand's-breadth of it shines alone
 'Mid the blank miles round about:

IV

For there I picked up on the heather
 And there I put inside my breast
A moulted feather, an eagle-feather!
 Well, I forget the rest.

EDWARD LEAR

(1812–1888, British)

The Owl and the Pussy Cat

The Owl and the Pussy-Cat went to sea
   In a beautiful pea-green boat.
They took some honey, and plenty of money
   Wrapped up in a five-pound note.
The Owl looked up to the stars above,
   And sang to a small guitar,
'O lovely Pussy! O Pussy, my love,
What a beautiful Pussy you are,
      You are,
      You are!
What a beautiful Pussy you are!'

Pussy said to the Owl, 'You elegant fowl!
   How charmingly sweet you sing!
O let us be married! too long we have tarried:
   But what shall we do for a ring?'
They sailed away, for a year and a day,
   To the land where the Bong-Tree grows,
And there in a wood a Piggy-wig stood,
With a ring at the end of his nose,
      His nose,
      His nose!
With a ring at the end of his nose.

'Dear Pig, are you willing to sell for one shilling
   Your ring?' Said the Piggy, 'I will.'

So they took it away, and were married next day
    By the Turkey who lives on the hill.
They dined on mince, and slices of quince,
    Which they ate with a runcible spoon;
And hand in hand, on the edge of the sand
    They danced by the light of the moon,
        The moon,
        The moon,
    They danced by the light of the moon.

EMILY OR CHARLOTTE BRONTË

(1818–1848, 1816–1855, British)

———

Stanzas

Often rebuked, yet always back returning
    To those first feelings that were born with me,
And leaving busy chase of wealth and learning
    For idle dreams of things which cannot be:

To-day, I will seek not the shadowy region;
    Its unsustaining vastness waxes drear,
And visions rising, legion after legion,
    Bring the unreal world too strangely near.

I'll walk, but not in old heroic traces,
    And not in paths of high morality,
And not among the half-distinguished faces,
    The clouded forms of long-past history.

I'll walk where my own nature would be leading:
    It vexes me to choose another guide:
Where the gray flocks in ferny glens are feeding,
    Where the wild wind blows on the mountain side.

What have those lonely mountains worth revealing?
    More glory and more grief than I can tell:
The earth that wakes *one* human heart to feeling
    Can centre both the worlds of Heaven and Hell.

HERMAN MELVILLE

(1819–1891, American)

———

The Maldive Shark

About the Shark, phlegmatical one,
Pale sot of the Maldive sea,
The sleek little pilot-fish, azure and slim,
How alert in attendance be.
From his saw-pit of mouth, from his charnel of maw
They have nothing of harm to dread,
But liquidly glide on his ghastly flank
Or before his Gorgonian head;
Or lurk in the port of serrated teeth
In white triple tiers of glittering gates,
And there find a haven when peril's abroad,
An asylum in jaws of the Fates!
They are friends; and friendly they guide him to prey,
Yet never partake of the treat —
Eyes and brains to the dotard lethargic and dull,
Pale ravener of horrible meat.

WALT WHITMAN

(1819–1892, American)

———

A Noiseless Patient Spider

A noiseless patient spider,
I mark'd where on a little promontory it stood isolated,
Mark'd how to explore the vacant vast surrounding,
It launch'd forth filament, filament, filament, out of itself,
Ever unreeling them, ever tirelessly speeding them.

And you O my soul where you stand,
Surrounded, detached, in measureless oceans of space,
Ceaselessly musing, venturing, throwing, seeking the
      spheres to connect them,
Till the bridge you will need be form'd, till the ductile
      anchor hold.
Till the gossamer thread you fling catch somewhere, O my
      soul.

DANTE GABRIEL ROSSETTI

(1828–1882, British)

———

The Woodspurge

The wind flapped loose, the wind was still,
Shaken out dead from tree and hill:
I had walked on at the wind's will, –
I sat now, for the wind was still.

Between my knees my forehead was, –
My lips, drawn in, said not Alas!
My hair was over in the grass,
My naked ears heard the day pass.

My eyes, wide open, had the run
Of some ten weeds to fix upon;
Among those few, out of the sun,
The woodspurge flowered, three cups in one.

From perfect grief there need not be
Wisdom or even memory:
One thing then learnt remains to me, –
The woodspurge has a cup of three.

EMILY DICKINSON

(1830–1886, American)

———

As imperceptibly as grief

As imperceptibly as grief
The summer lapsed away, –
Too imperceptible, at last,
To seem like perfidy.

A quietness distilled,
As twilight long begun,
Or Nature, spending with herself
Sequestered afternoon.

The dusk drew earlier in,
The morning foreign shone, –
A courteous, yet harrowing grace,
As guest who would be gone.

And thus, without a wing,
Or service of a keel,
Our summer made her light escape
Into the beautiful.

CHRISTINA ROSSETTI

(1830–1894, British)

———

When I am dead, my dearest

When I am dead, my dearest,
    Sing no sad songs for me;
Plant thou no roses at my head,
    Nor shady cypress tree:
Be the green grass above me
    With showers and dewdrops wet;
And if thou wilt, remember,
    And if thou wilt, forget.

I shall not see the shadows,
    I shall not feel the rain;
I shall not hear the nightingale
    Sing on, as if in pain:
And dreaming through the twilight
    That doth not rise nor set,
Haply I may remember,
    And haply may forget.

THOMAS HARDY

(1840–1928, British)

———

Afterwards

When the Present has latched its postern behind my
tremulous stay,
  And the May month flaps its glad green leaves like
wings,
Delicate-filmed as new-spun silk, will the neighbours say,
  'He was a man who used to notice such things'?

If it be in the dusk when, like an eyelid's soundless blink,
  The dewfall-hawk comes crossing the shades to alight
Upon the wind-warped upland thorn, a gazer may think,
  'To him this must have been a familiar sight.'

If I pass during some nocturnal blackness, mothy and
warm,
  When the hedgehog travels furtively over the lawn,
One may say, 'He strove that such innocent creatures
should come to no harm,
  But he could do little for them; and now he is gone.'

If, when hearing that I have been stilled at last, they stand
at the door,
  Watching the full-starred heavens that winter sees,
Will this thought rise on those who will meet my face no
more,
  'He was one who had an eye for such mysteries'?

And will any say when my bell of quittance is heard in the
     gloom,
   And a crossing breeze cuts a pause in its outrollings,
Till they rise again, as they were a new bell's boom,
   'He hears it not now, but used to notice such things'?

GERARD MANLEY HOPKINS

(1844–1889, British)

———

The Windhover

I caught this morning morning's minion, king-
  dom of daylight's dauphin, dapple-dawn-drawn Falcon,
    in his riding
  Of the rolling level underneath him steady air, and
    striding
High there, how he rung upon the rein of a wimpling
    wing
In his ecstasy! then off, off forth on swing,
  As a skate's heel sweeps smooth on a bow-bend: the
    hurl and gliding
  Rebuffed the big wind. My heart in hiding
Stirred for a bird,—the achieve of, the mastery of the
    thing!

Brute beauty and valour and act, oh, air, pride, plume,
    here
  Buckle! AND the fire that breaks from thee then, a
    billion
Times told lovelier, more dangerous, O my chevalier!

  No wonder of it: shéer plód makes plough down sillion
Shine, and blue-bleak embers, ah my dear,
  Fall, gall themselves, and gash gold-vermilion.

A. E. HOUSMAN

(1859–1936, British)

———

Into My Heart an Air that Kills

Into my heart an air that kills
  From yon far country blows:
What are those blue remembered hills,
  What spires, what farms are those?

That is the land of lost content,
  I see it shining plain,
The happy highways where I went
  And cannot come again.

RUDYARD KIPLING

(1865–1936, British)

———

The Way Through the Woods

They shut the road through the woods
Seventy years ago.
Weather and rain have undone it again,
And now you would never know
There was once a road through the woods
Before they planted the trees.
It is underneath the coppice and heath
And the thin anemones.
Only the keeper sees
That, where the ring-dove broods,
And the badgers roll at ease,
There was once a road through the woods,

Yet, if you enter the woods
Of a summer evening late,
When the night-air cools on the trout-ringed pools
Where the otter whistles his mate,
(They fear not men in the woods,
Because they see so few.)
You will hear the beat of a horse's feet,
And the swish of a skirt in the dew,
Steadily cantering through
The misty solitudes,
As though they perfectly knew
The old lost road through the woods. . . .
But there is no road through the woods.

WILLIAM BUTLER YEATS

(1865–1939, British)

Easter 1916

I have met them at close of day
Coming with vivid faces
From counter or desk among grey
Eighteenth-century houses.
I have passed with a nod of the head
Or polite meaningless words,
Or have lingered awhile and said
Polite meaningless words,
And thought before I had done
Of a mocking tale or a gibe
To please a companion
Around the fire at the club,
Being certain that they and I
But lived where motley is worn:
All changed, changed utterly:
A terrible beauty is born.

That woman's days were spent
In ignorant good-will,
Her nights in argument
Until her voice grew shrill.
What voice more sweet than hers
When, young and beautiful,
She rode to harriers?
This man had kept a school
And rode our wingèd horse;

This other his helper and friend
Was coming into his force;
He might have won fame in the end,
So sensitive his nature seemed,
So daring and sweet his thought.
This other man I had dreamed
A drunken, vainglorious lout.
He had done most bitter wrong
To some who are near my heart,
Yet I number him in the son;
He, too, has resigned his part
In the casual comedy;
He, too, has been changed in his turn,
Transformed utterly:
A terrible beauty is born.

Hearts with one purpose alone
Through summer and winter seem
Enchanted to a stone
To trouble the living stream.
The horse that comes from the road,
The rider, the birds that range
From cloud to tumbling cloud,
Minute by minute they change;
A shadow of cloud on the stream
Changes minute by minute;
A horse-hoof slides on the brim,
And a horse plashes within it;
The long-legged moor-hens dive,
And hens to moor-cocks call;
Minute by minute they live:
The stone's in the midst of all.

Too long a sacrifice
Can make a stone of the heart.
O when may it suffice?
That is Heaven's part, our part
To murmur name upon name,
As a mother names her child
When sleep at last has come
On limbs that had run wild
What is it but nightfall?
No, no, not night but death;
Was it needless death after all?
For England may keep faith
For all that is done and said.
We know their dream; enough
To know they dreamed and are dead;
And what if excess of love
Bewildered them till they died?
I write it out in a verse —
MacDonagh and MacBride
And Connolly and Pearse
Now and in time to be,
Wherever green is worn,
Are changed, changed utterly:
A terrible beauty is born.

EDWIN ARLINGTON ROBINSON

(1869–1935, American)

———

The House on the Hill

They are all gone away,
    The House is shut and still,
There is nothing more to say.

Through broken walls and gray
    The winds blow bleak and shrill:
They are all gone away.

Nor is there one to-day
    To speak them good or ill:
There is nothing more to say.

Why is it then we stray
    Around the sunken sill?
They are all gone away,

And our poor fancy-play
    For them is wasted skill:
There is nothing more to say.

There is ruin and decay
    In the House on the Hill:
They are all gone away,
There is nothing more to say.

STEPHEN CRANE

(1871–1900, American)

———

I saw a man pursuing the horizon

I saw a man pursuing the horizon;
Round and round they sped.
I was disturbed at this;
I accosted the man.
"It is futile," I said,
"You can never—"

"You lie," he cried,
And ran on.

PAUL LAWRENCE DUNBAR

(1872–1906, American)

Sympathy

I know what the caged bird feels, alas!
　When the sun is bright on the upland slopes;
When the wind stirs soft through the springing grass,
And the river flows like a stream of glass;
　When the first bird sings and the first bud opes,
And the faint perfume from its chalice steals—
I know what the caged bird feels!

I know why the caged bird beats his wing
　Till its blood is red on the cruel bars;
For he must fly back to his perch and cling
When he fain would be on the bough a-swing;
　And a pain still throbs in the old, old scars
And they pulse again with a keener sting—
I know why he beats his wing!

I know why the caged bird sings, ah me,
　When his wing is bruised and his bosom sore, —
When he beats his bars and he would be free;
It is not a carol of joy or glee,
　But a prayer that he sends from his heart's deep core,
But a plea, that upward to Heaven he flings—
I know why the caged bird sings!

ROBERT FROST

(1874–1963, American)

———

For Once, Then, Something

Others taunt me with having knelt at well-curbs
Always wrong to the light, so never seeing
Deeper down in the well than where the water
Gives me back in a shining surface picture
Me myself in the summer heaven godlike
Looking out of a wreath of fern and cloud puffs.
Once, when trying with chin against a well-curb,
I discerned, as I thought, beyond the picture,
Through the picture, a something white, uncertain,
Something more of the depths—and then I lost it.
Water came to rebuke the too clear water.
One drop fell from a fern, and lo, a ripple
Shook whatever it was lay there at bottom,
Blurred it, blotted it out. What was that whiteness?
Truth? A pebble of quartz? For once, then, something.

TRUMBULL STICKNEY

(1874–1904, American)

―――

Mnemosyne

It's autumn in the country I remember.

How warm a wind blew here about the ways!
And shadows on the hillside lay to slumber
During the long sun-sweetened summer-days.

It's cold abroad the country I remember.

The swallows veering skimmed the golden grain
At midday with a wing aslant and limber;
And yellow cattle browsed upon the plain.

It's empty down the country I remember.

I had a sister lovely in my sight:
Her hair was dark, her eyes were very sombre;
We sang together in the woods at night.

It's lonely in the country I remember.

The babble of our children fills my ears,
And on our hearth I stare the perished ember
To flames that show all starry thro' my tears.

It's dark about the country I remember.

There are the mountains where I lived. The path
Is slushed with cattle-tracks and fallen timber,
The stumps are twisted by the tempests' wrath.

But that I knew these places are my own,
I'd ask how came such wretchedness to cumber
The earth, and I to people it alone.

It rains across the country I remember.

EDWARD THOMAS

(1878–1917, American)

———

The Gallows

There was a weasel lived in the sun
With all his family,
Till a keeper shot him with his gun
And hung him up on a tree,
Where he swings in the wind and rain,
In the sun and in the snow,
Without pleasure, without pain,
On the dead oak tree bough.

There was a crow who was no sleeper,
But a thief and a murderer
Till a very late hour; and this keeper
Made him one of the things that were,
To hang and flap in rain and wind,
In the sun and in the snow.
There are no more sins to be sinned
On the dead oak tree bough.

There was a magpie, too,
Had a long tongue and a long tail;
He could both talk and do —
But what did that avail?
He, too, slaps in the wind and rain
Alongside weasel and crow,
Without pleasure, without pain,
On the dead oak tree bough.

[118]

And many other beasts
And birds, skin, bone, and feather,
Have been taken from their feasts
And hung up there together,
To swing and have endless leisure
In the sun and in the snow,
Without pain, without pleasure,
On the dead oak tree bough.

WALLACE STEVENS

(1879–1955, American)

———

A Postcard from the Volcano

Children picking up our bones
Will never know that these were once
As quick as foxes on the hill;

And that in autumn, when the grapes
Made sharp air sharper by their smell
These had a being, breathing frost;

And least will guess that with our bones
We left much more, left what still is
The look of things, left what we felt

At what we saw. The spring clouds blow
Above the shuttered mansion-house,
Beyond our gate and the windy sky

Cries out a literate despair.
We knew for long the mansion's look
And what we said of it became

A part of what it is . . . Children,
Still weaving budded aureoles,
Will speak our speech and never know.

Will say of the mansion that it seems
As if he that lived there left behind
A spirit storming in blank walls,

A dirty house in a gutted world,
A tatter of shadows peaked to white,
Smeared with the gold of the opulent sun.

WILLIAM CARLOS WILLIAMS

(1883–1963, American)

———

These

are the desolate, dark weeks
when nature in its barrenness
equals the stupidity of man.

The year plunges into night
and the heart plunges
lower than night

to an empty, windswept place
without sun, stars or moon
but a peculiar light as of thought

that spins a dark fire —
whirling upon itself until,
in the cold, it kindles

to make a man aware of nothing
that he knows, not loneliness
itself — Not a ghost but

would be embraced — emptiness,
despair — (They
whine and whistle) among

the flashes and booms of war;
houses of whose rooms
the cold is greater than can be thought,

the people gone that we loved,
the beds lying empty, the couches
damp, the chairs unused —

Hide it away somewhere
out of the mind, let it get roots
and grow, unrelated to jealous

ears and eyes — for itself.
In this mine they come to dig — all.
Is this the counterfoil to sweetest

music? The source of poetry that
seeing the clock stopped, says,
The clock has stopped

that ticked yesterday so well?
and hears the sound of lakewater
splashing — that is now stone.

D. H. LAWRENCE

(1885–1930, British)

———

Piano

Softly, in the dusk, a woman is singing to me;
Taking me back down the vista of years, till I see
A child sitting under the piano, in the boom of the tingling
     strings
And pressing the small, poised feet of a mother who smiles
     as she sings.

In spite of myself, the insidious mastery of song
Betrays me back, till the heart of me weeps to belong
To the old Sunday evenings at home, with winter outside
And hymns in the cosy parlour, the tinkling piano our
     guide.

So now it is vain for the singer to burst into clamour
With the great black piano appassionato. The glamour
Of childish days is upon me, my manhood is cast
Down in the flood of remembrance, I weep like a child for
     the past.

EZRA POUND

(1885–1972, American)

———

The River Merchant's Wife:
A Letter

While my hair was still cut straight across my forehead
I played about the front gate, pulling flowers.
You came by on bamboo stilts, playing horse,
You walked about my seat, playing with blue plums.
And we went on living in the village of Chokan:
Two small people, without dislike or suspicion.

At fourteen I married My Lord you.
I never laughed, being bashful.
Lowering my head, I looked at the wall.
Called to, a thousand times, I never looked back.

At fifteen I stopped scowling,
I desired my dust to be mingled with yours
Forever and forever and forever.
Why should I climb the look out?

At sixteen you departed,
You went into far Ku-tō-en, by the river of swirling
      eddies,
And you have been gone five months.
The monkeys make sorrowful noise overhead.

You dragged your feet when you went out.
By the gate now, the moss is grown, the different mosses,
Too deep to clear them away!
The leaves fall early this autumn, in wind.
The paired butterflies are already yellow with August

Over the grass in the West garden;
They hurt me. I grow older.
If you are coming down through the narrows of the river
        Kiang,
Please let me know beforehand,
And I will come out to meet you
            As far as Chō-fū-Sa.

EDWIN MUIR

(1887–1959, British)

―――

The Horses

Barely a twelvemonth after
The seven days war that put the world to sleep,
Late in the evening the strange horses came.
By then we had made our covenant with silence,
But in the first few days it was so still
We listened to our breathing and were afraid.
On the second day
The radios failed; we turned the knobs; no answer.
On the third day a warship passed us, heading north,
Dead bodies piled on the deck. On the sixth day
A plane plunged over us into the sea. Thereafter
Nothing. The radios dumb;
And still they stand in corners of our kitchens,
And stand, perhaps, turned on, in a million rooms
All over the world. But now if they should speak,
If on a sudden they should speak again,
If on the stroke of noon a voice should speak,
We would not listen, we would not let it bring
That old bad world that swallowed its children quick
At one great gulp. We would not have it again.
Sometimes we think of the nations lying asleep,
Curled blindly in impenetrable sorrow,
And then the thought confounds us with its strangeness.
The tractors lie about our fields; at evening
They look like dank sea-monsters couched and waiting.
We leave them where they are and let them rust:

"They'll molder away and be like other loam."
We make our oxen drag our rusty plows,
Long laid aside. We have gone back
Far past our fathers' land.

And then, that evening
Late in the summer the strange horses came.
We heard a distant tapping on the road,
A deepening drumming; it stopped, went on again
And at the corner changed to hollow thunder.
We saw the heads
Like a wild wave charging and were afraid.
We had sold our horses in our fathers' time
To buy new tractors. Now they were strange to us
As fabulous steeds set on an ancient shield
Or illustrations in a book of knights.
We did not dare go near them. Yet they waited,
Stubborn and shy, as if they had been sent
By an old command to find our whereabouts
And that long-lost archaic companionship.
In the first moment we had never a thought
That they were creatures to be owned and used.
Among them were some half a dozen colts
Dropped in some wilderness of the broken world,
Yet new as if they had come from their own Eden.
Since then they have pulled our plows and borne our
        loads,
But that free servitude still can pierce our hearts.
Our life is changed; their coming our beginning.

MARIANNE MOORE

(1887–1972, American)

———

A Grave

Man looking into the sea,
taking the view from those who have as much right to it
                                    as you have to it yourself,
it is human nature to stand in the middle of a thing,
but you cannot stand in the middle of this;
the sea has nothing to give but a well excavated grave.
The firs stand in a procession, each with an emerald
                                    turkey foot at the top,
reserved as their contours, saying nothing;
repression, however, is not the most obvious characteristic
        of the sea;
the sea is a collector, quick to return a rapacious look.
There are others besides you who have worn that look —
whose expression is no longer a protest; the fish no longer
                                    investigate them
for their bones have not lasted:
men lower nets, unconscious of the fact that they are
        desecrating a grave,
and row quickly away — the blades of the oars
moving together like the feet of water spiders as if there
        were no such thing as death.
The wrinkles progress among themselves in a phalanx —
        beautiful under networks of foam,
and fade breathlessly while the sea rustles in and out of
        the seaweed;
the birds swim through the air at top speed, emitting
                                    catcalls as heretofore —

the tortoise shell scourges about the feet of the cliffs, in
    motion beneath them;
and the ocean, under the pulsation of lighthouses and
    noise of bell buoys,
advances as usual, looking as if it were not that ocean in
    which dropped things are bound to sink —
in which if they turn and twist, it is neither with volition
    nor consciousness.

T. S. ELIOT

(1898–1965, British)

———

Animula

'Issues from the hand of God, the simple soul'
To a flat world of changing lights and noise,
To light, dark, dry or damp, chilly or warm;
Moving between the legs of tables and of chairs,
Rising or falling, grasping at kisses and toys,
Advancing boldly, sudden to take alarm,
Retreating to the corner of arm and knee,
Eager to be reassured, taking pleasure
In the fragrant brilliance of the Christmas tree,
Pleasure in the wind, the sunlight and the sea;
Studies the sunlit pattern on the floor
And running stags around a silver tray;
Confounds the actual and the fanciful,
Content with playing-cards and kings and queens,
What the fairies do and what the servants say.
The heavy burden of the growing soul
Perplexes and offends more, day by day;
Week by week, offends and perplexes more
With the imperatives of 'is and seems'
And may and may not, desire and control.
The pain of living and the drug of dreams
Curl up the small soul in the window seat
Behind the *Encyclopædia Britannica*.
Issues from the hand of time the simple soul
Irresolute and selfish, misshapen, lame,
Unable to fare forward or retreat,

Fearing the warm reality, the offered good,
Denying the importunity of the blood,
Shadow of its own shadows, spectre in its own gloom,
Leaving disordered papers in a dusty room;
Living first in the silence after the viaticum.

Pray for Guiterriez, avid of speed and power,
For Boudin, blown to pieces,
For this one who made a great fortune,
And that one who went his own way.
Pray for Floret, by the boarhound slain between the yew
        trees,
Pray for us now and at the hour of our birth.

CONRAD AIKEN

(1889–1973, American)

———

Annihilation

While the blue noon above us arches,
And the poplar sheds disconsolate leaves,
Tell me again why love bewitches,
And what love gives.

Is it the trembling finger that traces
The eyebrow's curve, the curve of the cheek?
The mouth that quivers, when the hand caresses,
But cannot speak?

No, not these, not in these is hidden
The secret, more than in other things:
Not only the touch of a hand can gladden
Till the blood sings.

It is the leaf that falls between us,
The bells that murmur, the shadows that move,
The autumnal sunlight that fades upon us:
These things are love.

It is the 'No, let us sit here longer,'
The 'Wait till tomorrow,' the 'Once I knew —'
These trifles, said as I touch your finger,
And the clock strikes two.

The world is intricate, and we are nothing.
It is the complex world of grass,
A twig on the path, a look of loathing,
Feelings that pass —

These are the secret! And I could hate you,
When, as I lean for another kiss,
I see in your eyes that I do not meet you,
And that love is this.

Rock meeting rock can know love better
Than eyes that stare or lips that touch.
All that we know in love is bitter,
And it is not much.

EDNA ST. VINCENT MILLAY

(1892–1950, American)

———

What lips my lips have kissed, and where, and why

What lips my lips have kissed, and where, and why,
I have forgotten, and what arms have lain
Under my head till morning; but the rain
Is full of ghosts tonight, that tap and sigh
Upon the glass and listen for reply,
And in my heart there stirs a quiet pain
For unremembered lads that not again
Will turn to me at midnight with a cry.
Thus in the winter stands the lonely tree,
Nor knows what birds have vanished one by one,
Yet knows its boughs more silent than before:
I cannot say what loves have come and gone,
I only know that summer sang in me
A little while, that in me sings no more.

ARCHIBALD MacLEISH

(1892–1982, American)

———

You, Andrew Marvell

And here face down beneath the sun
And here upon earth's noonward height
To feel the always coming on
The always rising of the night:

To feel creep up the curving east
The earthly chill of dusk and slow
Upon those under lands the vast
And ever climbing shadow grow

And strange at Ecbatan the trees
Take leaf by leaf the evening strange
The flooding dark about their knees
The mountains over Persia change

And now at Kermanshah the gate
Dark empty and the withered grass
And through the twilight now the late
Few travelers in the westward pass

And Baghdad darken and the bridge
Across the silent river gone
And through Arabia the edge
Of evening widen and steal on

And deepen on Palmyra's street
The wheel rut in the ruined stone
And Lebanon fade out and Crete
High through the clouds and overblown

And over Sicily the air
Still flashing with the landward gulls
And loom and slowly disappear
The sails above the shadowy hulls

And Spain go under and the shore
Of Africa the gilded sand
And evening vanish and no more
The low pale light across the land

Nor now the long light on the sea:

And here face downward in the sun
To feel how swift how secretly
The shadow of the night comes on . . .

WILFRED OWEN

(1893–1918, British)

——

Anthem for Doomed Youth

What passing-bells for these who die as cattle?
  — Only the monstrous anger of the guns.
  Only the stuttering rifles' rapid rattle
Can patter out their hasty orisons.
No mockeries now for them; no prayers nor bells;
  Nor any voice of mourning save the choirs, —
The shrill, demented choirs of wailing shells;
  And bugles calling for them from sad shires.

What candles may be held to speed them all?
  Not in the hands of boys but in their eyes
Shall shine the holy glimmers of goodbyes.
  The pallor of girls' brows shall be their pall;
Their flowers the tenderness of patient minds,
And each slow dusk a drawing-down of blinds.

HART CRANE

(1899–1932, American)

Repose of Rivers

The willows carried a slow sound,
A sarabande the wind mowed on the mead.
I could never remember
That seething, steady leveling of the marshes
Till age had brought me to the sea.

Flags, weeds. And remembrance of steep alcoves
Where cypresses shared the noon's
Tyranny; they drew me into hades almost.
And mammoth turtles climbing sulphur dreams
Yielded, while sun-silt rippled them
Asunder . . .

How much I would have bartered! the black gorge
And all the singular nestings in the hills
Where beavers learn stitch and tooth.
The pond I entered once and quickly fled —
I remember now its singing willow rim.

And finally, in that memory all things nurse;
After the city that I finally passed
With scalding unguents spread and smoking darts
The monsoon cut across the delta
At gulf gates . . . There, beyond the dykes

I heard wind flaking sapphire, like this summer,
And willows could not hold more steady sound.

LANGSTON HUGHES

(1902–1967, American)

Advice

Folks, I'm telling you,
birthing is hard
and dying is mean —
so get yourself
a little loving
in between.

COUNTEE CULLEN

(1903–1946, American)

―――

Yet Do I Marvel

I doubt not God is good, well-meaning, kind,
And did He stoop to quibble could tell why
The little buried mole continues blind,
Why flesh that mirrors Him must some day die,
Make plain the reason tortured Tantalus
Is baited by the fickle fruit, declare
If merely brute caprice dooms Sisyphus
To struggle up a never-ending stair.
Inscrutable His ways are, and immune
To catechism by a mind too strewn
With petty cares to slightly understand
What awful brain compels His awful hand.
Yet do I marvel at this curious thing:
To make a poet black, and bid him sing!

ROBERT PENN WARREN

(1905–1989, American)

———

Birth of Love

Season late, day late, sun just down, and the sky
Cold gunmetal but with a wash of live rose, and she,
From water the color of sky except where
Her motion has fractured it to shivering splinters of silver,
Rises. Stands on the raw grass. Against
The new-curdling night of spruces, nakedness
Glimmers and, at bosom and flank, drips
With fluent silver. The man,

Some ten strokes out, but now hanging
Motionless in the gunmetal water, feet
Cold with the coldness of depth, all
History dissolving from him, is
Nothing but an eye. Is an eye only. Sees

The body that is marked by his use, and Time's,
Rise, and in the abrupt and unsustaining element of air,
Sway, lean, grapple the pond-bank. Sees
How, with that posture of female awkwardness that is,
And is the stab of, suddenly perceived grace, breasts bulge
     down in
The pure curve of their weight and buttocks
Moon up and, in that swelling unity,
Are silver, and glimmer. Then

[142]

The body is erect, she is herself, whatever
Self she may be, and with an end of the towel grasped in
            each hand,
Slowly draws it back and forth across back and buttocks,
            but
With face lifted toward the high sky, where
The over-wash of rose color now fails. Fails, though no
            star
Yet throbs there. The towel, forgotten,
Does not move now. The gaze
Remains fixed on the sky. The body,

Profiled against the darkness of spruces, seems
To draw to itself, and condense in its whiteness, what light
In the sky yet lingers or, from
The metallic and abstract severity of water, lifts. The
            body,
With the towel now trailing loose from one hand, is
A white stalk from which the face flowers gravely toward
            the high sky.
This moment is non-sequential and absolute, and admits
Of no definition, for it
Subsumes all other, and sequential, moments, by which
Definition might be possible. The woman,

Face yet raised, wraps,
With a motion as though standing in sleep,
The towel about her body, under the breasts, and,
Holding it there, hieratic as lost Egypt and erect,
Moves up the path that, stair-steep, winds
Into the clamber and tangle of growth. Beyond
The lattice of dusk-dripping leaves, whiteness
Dimly glimmers, goes. Glimmers and is gone, and the
            man,

Suspended in his darkling medium, stares
Upward where, though not visible, he knows
She moves, and in his heart he cries out that, if only
He had such strength, he would put his hand forth
And maintain it over her to guard, in all
Her out-goings and in-comings, from whatever
Inclemency of sky or slur of the world's weather
Might ever be. In his heart
He cries out. Above

Height of the spruce-night and heave of the far mountain,
        he sees
The first star pulse into being. It gleams there.

I do not know what promise it makes to him.

W. H. AUDEN

(1907–1973, American)

In Memory of W. B. Yeats

I

He disappeared in the dead of winter:
The brooks were frozen, the airports almost deserted,
And snow disfigured the public statues;
The mercury sank in the mouth of the dying day.
What instruments we have agree
The day of his death was a dark cold day.

Far from his illness
The wolves ran on through the evergreen forests,
The peasant river was untempted by the fashionable
       quays;
By mourning tongues
The death of the poet was kept from his poems.

But for him it was his last afternoon as himself,
An afternoon of nurses and rumours;
The provinces of his body revolted,
The squares of his mind were empty,
Silence invaded the suburbs,
The current of his feeling failed; he became his admirers.

Now he is scattered among a hundred cities
And wholly given over to unfamiliar affections,
To find his happiness in another kind of wood

And be punished under a foreign code of conscience.
The words of a dead man
Are modified in the guts of the living.

But in the importance and noise of to-morrow
When the brokers are roaring like beasts on the floor of
      the Bourse,
And the poor have the sufferings to which they are fairly
      accustomed,
And each in the cell of himself is almost convinced of his
      freedom,
A few thousand will think of this day
As one thinks of a day when one did something slightly
      unusual.
What instruments we have agree
The day of his death was a dark cold day.

II

    You were silly like us; your gift survived it all:
    The parish of rich women, physical decay,
    Yourself. Mad Ireland hurt you into poetry.
    Now Ireland has her madness and her weather
      still,
    For poetry makes nothing happen: it survives
    In the valley of its making where executives
    Would never want to tamper, flows on south
    From ranches of isolation and the busy griefs,
    Raw towns that we believe and die in; it
      survives,
    A way of happening, a mouth.

III

Earth, receive an honoured guest:
William Yeats is laid to rest.
Let the Irish vessel lie
Emptied of its poetry.

In the nightmare of the dark
All the dogs of Europe bark,
And the living nations wait,
Each sequestered in its hate;

Intellectual disgrace
Stares from every human face,
And the seas of pity lie
Locked and frozen in each eye.

Follow, poet, follow right
To the bottom of the night,
With your unconstraining voice
Still persuade us to rejoice;

With the farming of a verse
Make a vineyard of the curse,
Sing of human unsuccess
In a rapture of distress;

In the deserts of the heart
Let the healing fountain start,
In the prison of his days
Teach the free man how to praise.

A. D. HOPE

(1907–   , Australian)

———

Observation Car

To be put on the train and kissed and given my ticket,
Then the station slid blackward, the shops and the neon
    lighting,
Reeling off in a drunken blur, with a whole pound note in
    my pocket
And the holiday packed with Perhaps. It used to be very
    exciting.

The present and past were enough. I did not mind having
    my back
To the engine. I sat like a spider and spun
Time backward out of my guts – or rather my eyes – and
    the track
Was a Now dwindling off to oblivion. I thought it was fun:

The telegraph poles slithered up in a sudden crescendo
As we sliced the hill and scattered its grazing sheep;
The days were a wheeling delirium that led without end to
Nights when we plunged into roaring tunnels of sleep.

But now I am tired of the train. I have learned that one
    tree
Is much like another, one hill the dead spit of the next
I have seen trailing off behind all the various types of
    country
Like a clock running down. I am bored and a little
    perplexed;

And weak with the effort of endless evacuation
Of the long monotonous Now, the repetitive, tidy
Officialdom of each siding, of each little station
Labelled Monday, Tuesday — and goodness! what
        happened to Friday?

And the maddening way the other passengers alter:
The schoolgirl who goes to the Ladies' comes back to her
        seat
A lollipop blonde who leads you on to assault her,
And you've just got her skirts round her waist and her
        pants round her feet

When you find yourself fumbling about the nightmare
        knees
Of a pink hippopotamus with a permanent wave
Who sends you for sandwiches and a couple of teas,
But by then she has whiskers, no teeth and one foot in the
        grave.

I have lost my faith that the ticket tells where we are
        going.
There are rumours the driver is mad — we are all being
        trucked
To the abattoirs somewhere — the signals are jammed and
        unknowing
We aim through the night full speed at a wrecked viaduct.

But I do not believe them. The future is rumour and
        drivel;
Only the past is assured. From the observation car
I stand looking back and watching the landscape shrivel,
Wondering where we are going and just where the hell we
        are,

Remembering how I planned to break the journey, to
     drive
My own car one day, to have choice in my hands and my
     foot upon power,
To see through the trumpet throat of vertiginous
     perspective
My urgent Now explode continually into flower,

To be the Eater of Time, a poet and not that sly
Anus of mind the historian. It was so simple and plain
To live by the sole, insatiable influx of the eye.
But something went wrong with the plan: I am still on the
     train.

LOUIS MacNEICE

(1907–1963, British)

———

The Brandy Glass

Only let it form within his hands once more –
The moment cradled like a brandy glass.
Sitting alone in the empty dining hall . . .
From the chandeliers the snow begins to fall
Piling around carafes and table legs
And chokes the passage of the revolving door.
The last diner, like a ventriloquist's doll
Left by his master, gazes before him, begs:
'Only let it form within my hands once more.'

ELIZABETH BISHOP

(1911–1979, American)

———

At the Fishhouses

Although it is a cold evening,
down by one of the fishhouses
an old man sits netting,
his net, in the gloaming almost invisible
a dark purple-brown,
and his shuttle worn and polished.
The air smells so strong of codfish
it makes one's nose run and one's eyes water.
The five fishhouses have steeply peaked roofs
and narrow, cleated gangplanks slant up
to storerooms in the gables
for the wheelbarrows to be pushed up and down on.
All is silver: the heavy surface of the sea,
swelling slowly as if considering spilling over,
is opaque, but the silver of the benches,
the lobster pots, and masts, scattered
among the wild jagged rocks,
is of an apparent translucence
like the small old buildings with an emerald moss
growing on their shoreward walls.
The big fish tubs are completely lined
with layers of beautiful herring scales
and the wheelbarrows are similarly plastered
with creamy iridescent coats of mail,
with small iridescent flies crawling on them.
Up on the little slope behind the houses,

set in the sparse bright sprinkle of grass,
is an ancient wooden capstan,
cracked, with two long bleached handles
and some melancholy stains, like dried blood,
where the ironwork has rusted.
The old man accepts a Lucky Strike.
He was a friend of my grandfather.
We talk of the decline in the population
and of codfish and herring
while he waits for a herring boat to come in.
There are sequins on his vest and on his thumb.
He has scraped the scales, the principal beauty,
from unnumbered fish with that black old knife,
the blade of which is almost worn away.

Down at the water's edge, at the place
where they haul up the boats, up the long ramp
descending into the water, thin silver
tree trunks are laid horizontally
across the gray stones, down and down
at intervals of four or five feet.

Cold dark deep and absolutely clear,
element bearable to no mortal,
to fish and to seals . . . One seal particularly
I have seen here evening after evening.
He was curious about me. He was interested in music;
like me a believer in total immersion,
so I used to sing him Baptist hymns.
I also sang "A Mighty Fortress Is Our God."
He stood up in the water and regarded me
steadily, moving his head a little.
Then he would disappear, then suddenly emerge
almost in the same spot, with a sort of shrug
as if it were against his better judgment.

Cold dark deep and absolutely clear,
the clear gray icy water . . . Back, behind us,
the dignified tall firs begin.
Bluish, associating with their shadows,
a million Christmas trees stand
waiting for Christmas. The water seems suspended
above the rounded gray and blue-gray stones.
I have seen it over and over, the same sea, the same,
slightly, indifferently swinging above the stones,
icily free above the stones,
above the stones and then the world.
If you should dip your hand in,
your wrist would ache immediately,
your bones would begin to ache and your hand would
        burn
as if the water were a transmutation of fire
that feeds on stones and burns with a dark gray flame.
If you tasted it, it would first taste bitter,
then briny, then surely burn your tongue.
It is like what we imagine knowledge to be:
dark, salt, clear, moving, utterly free,
drawn from the cold hard mouth
of the world, derived from the rocky breasts
forever, flowing and drawn, and since
our knowledge is historical, flowing, and flown.

ROBERT HAYDEN

(1913–1980, American)

———

Those Winter Sundays

Sundays too my father got up early
and put his clothes on in the blueblack cold,
then with cracked hands that ached
from labor in the weekday weather made
banked fires blaze. No one ever thanked him.

I'd wake and hear the cold splintering, breaking.
When the rooms were warm, he'd call,
and slowly I would rise and dress,
fearing the chronic angers of that house,

Speaking indifferently to him,
who had driven out the cold
and polished my good shoes as well.
What did I know, what did I know
of love's austere and lonely offices?

JOHN BERRYMAN

(1914–1972, American)

———

The Moon and the Night and the Men

On the night of the Belgian surrender the moon rose
Late, a delayed moon, and a violent moon
For the English or the American beholder;
The French beholder. It was a cold night,
People put on their wraps, the troops were cold
No doubt, despite the calendar, no doubt
Numbers of refugees coughed, and the sight
Or sound of some killed others. A cold night.

On Outer Drive there was an accident:
A stupid well-intentioned man turned sharp
Right and abruptly he became an angel
Fingering an unfamiliar harp,
Or screamed in hell, or was nothing at all.
Do not imagine this is unimportant.
He was a part of the night, part of the land,
Part of the bitter and exhausted ground
Out of which memory grows.

                    Michael and I
Stared at each other over chess, and spoke
As little as possible, and drank and played.
The chessmen caught in the European eye,
Neither of us I think had a free look
Although the game was fair. The move one made
It was difficult at last to keep one's mind on.

'Hurt and unhappy' said the man in London.
We said to each other, The time is coming near
When none shall have books or music, none his dear,
And only a fool will speak aloud his mind.
History is approaching a speechless end,
As Henry Adams said. Adams was right.

All this occurred on the night when Leopold
Fulfilled the treachery four years before
Begun — or was he well-intentioned, more
Roadmaker to hell than king? At any rate,
The moon came up late and the night was cold,
Many men died — although we know the fate
Of none, nor of anyone, and the war
Goes on, and the moon in the breast of man is cold.

DYLAN THOMAS

(1914–1953, British)

———

Fern Hill

Now as I was young and easy under the apple boughs
About the lilting house and happy as the grass was green,
   The night above the dingle starry,
     Time let me hail and climb
   Golden in the heydays of his eyes,
And honoured among wagons I was prince of the apple
        towns
And once below a time I lordly had the trees and leaves
     Trail with daisies and barley
   Down the rivers of the windfall light.

And as I was green and carefree, famous among the barns
About the happy yard and singing as the farm was home,
   In the sun that is young once only,
     Time let me play and be
   Golden in the mercy of his means,
And green and golden I was huntsman and herdsman, the
        calves
Sang to my horn, the foxes on the hills barked clear and
        cold,
     And the sabbath rang slowly
   In the pebbles of the holy streams.

All the sun long it was running, it was lovely, the hay
Fields high as the house, the tunes from the chimneys, it
        was air

And playing, lovely and watery
    And fire green as grass.
And nightly under the simple stars
As I rode to sleep the owls were bearing the farm away,
All the moon long I heard, blessed among stables, the
        nightjars
    Flying with the ricks, and the horses
      Flashing into the dark.

And then to awake, and the farm, like a wanderer white
With the dew, come back, the cock on his shoulder: it was
    all
    Shining, it was Adam and maiden,
      The sky gathered again
    And the sun grew round that very day.
So it must have been after the birth of the simple light
In the first, spinning place, the spellbound horses walking
        warm
    Out of the whinnying green stable
      On to the fields of praise.

And honoured among foxes and pheasants by the gay
        house
Under the new made clouds and happy as the heart was
        long,
    In the sun born over and over,
      I ran my heedless ways,
    My wishes raced through the house high hay
And nothing I cared, at my sky blue trades, that time
        allows
In all his tuneful turning so few and such morning songs
    Before the children green and golden
      Follow him out of grace,

Nothing I cared, in the lamb white days, that time would
        take me

Up to the swallow thronged loft by the shadow of my
      hand,
  In the moon that is always rising,
    Nor that riding to sleep
  I should hear him fly with the high fields
And wake to the farm forever fled from the childless land.
Oh as I was young and easy in the mercy of his means,
    Time held me green and dying
  Though I sang in my chains like the sea.

ROBERT LOWELL

(1917–1977, American)

Fall 1961

Back and forth, back and forth
goes the tock, tock, tock
of the orange, bland, ambassadorial
face of the moon
on the grandfather clock.

All autumn, the chafe and jar
of nuclear war;
we have talked our extinction to death.
I swim like a minnow
behind my studio window.

Our end drifts nearer,
the moon lifts,
radiant with terror.
The state
is a diver under a glass bell.

A father's no shield
for his child.
We are like a lot of wild
spiders crying together,
but without tears.

Nature holds up a mirror.
One swallow makes a summer.
It's easy to tick
off the minutes,
but the clockhands stick.

Back and forth!
Back and forth, back and forth —
my one point of rest
is the orange and black
oriole's swinging nest!

AMY CLAMPITT

(1920–   , American)

Meridian

First daylight on the bittersweet-hung
sleeping porch at high summer : dew
all over the lawn, sowing diamond-
point-highlighted shadows :
the hired man's shadow revolving
along the walk, a flash of milkpails
passing : no threat in sight, no hint
anywhere in the universe, of that

apathy at the meridian, the noon
of absolute boredom : flies
crooning black lullabies in the kitchen,
milk-soured crocks, cream separator
still unwashed : what is there to life
but chores and more chores, dishwater,
fatigue, unwanted children : nothing
to stir the longueur of afternoon

except possibly thunderheads :
climbing, livid, turreted alabaster
lit up from within by splendor and terror
—forked lightning's
               split-second disaster.

GWEN HARWOOD

(1920–   , Australian)

——

In the Park

She sits in the park. Her clothes are out of date.
Two children whine and bicker, tug her skirt.
A third draws aimless patterns in the dirt.
Someone she loved once passes by — too late

to feign indifference to that casual nod.
"How nice," et cetera. "Time holds great surprises."
From his neat head unquestionably rises
a small balloon . . . "but for the grace of God . . ."

They stand a while in flickering light, rehearsing
the children's names and birthdays. "It's so sweet
to hear their chatter, watch them grow and thrive,"
she says to his departing smile. Then, nursing
the youngest child, sits staring at her feet.
To the wind she says, "They have eaten me alive."

RICHARD WILBUR

(1921–   , American)

───

Advice to a Prophet

When you come, as you soon must, to the streets of our
      city,
Mad-eyed from stating the obvious,
Not proclaiming our fall but begging us
In God's name to have self-pity,

Spare us all word of the weapons, their force and range,
The long numbers that rocket the mind;
Our slow, unreckoning hearts will be left behind,
Unable to fear what is too strange.

Nor shall you scare us with talk of the death of the race.
How should we dream of this place without us? —
The sun mere fire, the leaves untroubled about us,
A stone look on the stone's face?

Speak of the world's own change. Though we cannot
      conceive
Of an undreamt thing, we know to our cost
How the dreamt cloud crumbles, the vines are blackened
      by frost,
How the view alters. We could believe,

If you told us so, that the white-tailed deer will slip
Into perfect shade, grown perfectly shy,
The lark avoid the reaches of our eye,
The jack-pine lose its knuckled grip

On the cold ledge, and every torrent burn
As Xanthus once, its gliding trout
Stunned in a twinkling. What should we be without
The dolphin's arc, the dove's return,

These things in which we have seen ourselves and
        spoken?
Ask us, prophet, how we shall call
Our natures forth when that live tongue is all
Dispelled, that glass obscured or broken

In which we have said the rose of our love and the clean
Horse of our courage, in which beheld
The singing locust of the soul unshelled,
And all we mean or wish to mean.

Ask us, ask us whether with the worldless rose
Our hearts shall fail us; come demanding
Whether there shall be lofty or long standing
When the bronze annals of the oak-tree close.

PHILIP LARKIN

(1922–1985, British)

———

Aubade

I work all day, and get half-drunk at night.
Waking at four to soundless dark, I stare.
In time the curtain-edges will grow light.
Till then I see what's really always there:
Unresting death, a whole day nearer now,
Making all thought impossible but how
And where and when I shall myself die.
Arid interrogation: yet the dread
Of dying, and being dead,
Flashes afresh to hold and horrify.

The mind blanks at the glare. Not in remorse
– The good not done, the love not given, time
Torn off unused – nor wretchedly because
An only life can take so long to climb
Clear of its wrong beginnings, and may never;
But at the total emptiness for ever,
The sure extinction that we travel to
And shall be lost in always. Not to be here,
Not to be anywhere,
And soon; nothing more terrible, nothing more true.

This is a special way of being afraid
No trick dispels. Religion used to try,
That vast moth-eaten musical brocade
Created to pretend we never die,

And specious stuff that says *No rational being*
Can fear a thing it will not feel, not seeing
That this is what we fear—no sight, no sound,
No touch or taste or smell, nothing to think with,
Nothing to love or link with,
The anaesthetic from which none come round.

And so it stays just on the edge of vision,
A small unfocused blur, a standing chill
That slows each impulse down to indecision.
Most things may never happen: this one will,
And realisation of it rages out
In furnace-fear when we are caught without
People or drink. Courage is no good:
It means not scaring others. Being brave
Lets no one off the grave.
Death is no different whined at than withstood.

Slowly light strengthens, and the room takes shape.
It stands plain as a wardrobe, what we know,
Have always known, know that we can't escape,
Yet can't accept. One side will have to go.
Meanwhile telephones crouch, getting ready to ring
In locked-up offices, and all the uncaring
Intricate rented world begins to rouse.
The sky is white as clay, with no sun.
Work has to be done.
Postmen like doctors go from house to house.

HOWARD MOSS

(1922–1987, American)

———

Ménage à Trois

Another sunset of scrambled eggs
And wine, Mars under the piano, laughing,
Venus at the door of the frigidaire,
Saying, "We're all out of blood again!"
How I deplore her use of the language!
You ask how we get along? Not well.
Temperamental discrepancies:
Her habit of saying nothing grandly,
His fake interest in the cause of things.
The food is dreadful. The weather worse.
So much for all the touted joys
Of the Riviera — or wherever we are.
The dullness of the nights is hard to believe,
Though, from outside, I gather we cause
A sensation. Who's sleeping with whom?
We keep them guessing: Nobody is.
The schedule goes something like this:
She works on her cookbook, "Venus Cooks,"
He works part time at the Peace Foundation.
And I start out — well, you know me:
I rip through the Debussy Preludes, shave,
Feel ashamed at detesting travel,
Read, write, go for a walk, and think —
Not that there's much here to think about.
Lunch, usually mushrooms picked
By the local mushroom maniac, whom

We trust, *ça va sans dire*, then back
To my desk for a note or two, more work,
He comes home, she *in* from the gazebo,
Where she writes — and then it's cocktail time!
Singapore slings served in jelly glasses,
Both à la mode in nineteen thirty-nine
(That's the year the Spanish War closed down).
To say I was bored would overstate the case.
I'm languid. They're worse. Desultory.

Of course, he's nineteen, and has fresh thoughts,
She *can* be amusing. At dusk, on the terrace,
I get myself up like a Chinese sage,
My bathrobe from Brooks dyed raven blue,
And we talk of our Oedipal strangulations —
Each so different and each the same.
Later, we provide pornography
(Mental) for the neighbors, who watch our blinds
As if they were about to disclose an orgy,
Something worthy of the TV sets
They hunch over like a herd of cattle.
Then, with a little citrus kiss goodnight,
We part, and so the days go by. . . .

We're followed to the market by a limousine,
Green, a Rolls, in which an assassin
Is discreetly invisible in the back seat.
So we say. It's probably the victim.
I have come to believe in loneliness,
Disguised as it is as an optical illusion.
Rumors are rife: something rose from the sea,
Somebody saw a stain of blood —
But, no matter what they say, the sun's the same.
This morning, I wrote, beginning a poem,
"That sedative, the sun" — but I couldn't go on.

They're at the door. Another game.
She: (Screaming) "Leave me *alone!*"
He: "Tonight, we'll really go to town."
You want my view of the whole situation?
It's old, inadequate, and flourishing.

ANTHONY HECHT

(1923–   , American)

———

A Hill

In Italy, where this sort of thing can occur,
I had a vision once – though you understand
It was nothing at all like Dante's, or the visions of saints,
And perhaps not a vision at all. I was with some friends,
Picking my way through a warm sunlit piazza
In the early morning. A clear fretwork of shadows
From huge umbrellas littered the pavement and made
A sort of lucent shallows in which was moored
A small navy of carts. Books, coins, old maps,
Cheap landscapes and ugly religious prints
Were all on sale. The colors and noise
Like the flying hands were gestures of exultation,
So that even the bargaining
Rose to the ear like a voluble godliness.
And then, when it happened, the noises suddenly stopped,
And it got darker; pushcarts and people dissolved
And even the great Farnese Palace itself
Was gone, for all its marble; in its place
Was a hill, mole-colored and bare. It was very cold,
Close to freezing, with a promise of snow.
The trees were like old ironwork gathered for scrap
Outside a factory wall. There was no wind,
And the only sound for a while was the little click
Of ice as it broke in the mud under my feet.
I saw a piece of ribbon snagged on a hedge,
But no other sign of life. And then I heard

What seemed the crack of a rifle. A hunter, I guessed;
At least I was not alone. But just after that
Came the soft and papery crash
Of a great branch somewhere unseen falling to earth.

And that was all, except for the cold and silence
That promised to last forever, like the hill.

Then prices came through, and fingers, and I was restored
To the sunlight and my friends. But for more than a week
I was scared by the plain bitterness of what I had seen.
All this happened about ten years ago,
And it hasn't troubled me since, but at last, today,
I remembered that hill; it lies just to the left
Of the road north of Poughkeepsie; and as a boy
I stood before it for hours in wintertime.

JOHN ASHBERY

(1927–   , American)

———

As You Came from the Holy Land

of western New York state
were the graves all right in their bushings
was there a note of panic in the late August air
because the old man had peed in his pants again
was there turning away from the late afternoon glare
as though it too could be wished away
was any of this present
and how could this be
the magic solution to what you are in now
whatever has held you motionless
like this so long through the dark season
until now the women come out in navy blue
and the worms come out of the compost to die
it is the end of any season

you reading there so accurately
sitting not wanting to be disturbed
as you came from that holy land
what other signs of earth's dependency were upon you
what fixed sign at the crossroads
what lethargy in the avenues
where all is said in a whisper
what tone of voice among the hedges
what tone under the apple trees
the numbered land stretches away
and your house is built in tomorrow

but surely not before the examination
of what is right and will befall
not before the census
and the writing down of names

remember you are free to wander away
as from other times other scenes that were taking place
the history of someone who came too late
the time is ripe now and the adage
is hatching as the seasons change and tremble
it is finally as though that thing of monstrous interest
were happening in the sky
but the sun is setting and prevents you from seeing it

out of night the token emerges
its leaves like birds alighting all at once under a tree
taken up and shaken again
put down in weak rage
knowing as the brain does it can never come about
not here not yesterday in the past
only in the gap of today filling itself
as emptiness is distributed
in the idea of what time it is
when that time is already past

COPYRIGHT ACKNOWLEDGMENTS

About the Editor

Mark Strand was born in Summerside, Prince Edward Island, Canada, and was raised and educated in the United States and South America. He is the author of eight books of poems, the most recent of which is *Dark Harbor,* published in 1993. His book of short stories, *Mr. and Mrs. Baby* was published in 1985. His translations include *The Owl's Insomnia,* a selection of Rafael Alberti's poems, and *Travelling in the Family,* a selection of Carlos Drummond de Andrade's poems, edited in collaboration with Thomas Colchie. He has written several children's books, and edited several anthologies, including *Another Republic,* which he co-edited with Charles Simic. He has published numerous articles and essays on painting and photography, most recently, *Hopper,* in 1994. He has been the recipient of fellowships from the Ingram Merrill, Rockefeller and Guggenheim Foundations and from the National Endowment for the Arts. In 1979 he was awarded the Fellowship of the Academy of American Poets, and in 1987 he received a John D. and Catherine T. MacArthur Fellowship. In 1990 he was chosen by the Librarian of Congress to be Poet Laureate of the United States. He lives in Baltimore with his wife and son.